The It Factor: What Makes a Teacher Great?

Advances in Teaching and Teacher Education

VOLUME 2

Series Editor

Yeping Li, *Texas A&M University, College Station, USA*

International Advisory Board

Miriam Ben-Peretz, *University of Haifa, Israel*
Cheryl J. Craig, *University of Houston, USA*
Jennifer Gore, *University of Newcastle, Australia*
Stephanie L. Knight, *Pennsylvania State University, USA*
Allen Yuk Lun Leung, *Hong Kong Baptist University, Hong Kong*
Ian Menter, *University of Oxford, UK*
Yolanda N. Padrón, *Texas A&M University, USA*
Hersh C. Waxman, *Texas A&M University, USA*

Scope

Advances in Teaching and Teacher Education is an international book series that aims to provide an important outlet for sharing the state-of-the-art research, knowledge, and practices of teaching and teacher education. The series helps promote the discussion, improvement, and assessment of teachers' quality, teaching, and instructional innovations including technology integration at all school levels as well as through teacher education around the world. With no specific restriction to disciplines, the series strives to address and synthesize different aspects and stages in teaching and teacher professional development both within and across disciplines, various interactions throughout the process of instructional activities and teacher education from various theoretical, policy, psychological, socio-cultural, or cross-cultural perspectives. The series features books that are contributed by researchers, teacher educators, instructional specialists, and practitioners from different education systems.

The titles published in this series are listed at *brill.com/atte*

The It Factor: What Makes a Teacher Great?

By

Holly J. Thornton

BRILL

SENSE

LEIDEN | BOSTON

All chapters in this book have undergone peer review.

The Library of Congress Cataloging-in-Publication Data is available online at http://catalog.loc.gov

Names: Thornton, Holly J., author.
Title: The it factor : what makes a teacher great? / By Holly J. Thornton.
Description: Leiden; Boston : Brill Sense, [2018] | Series: Advances in teaching and
    teacher education ; 2 | Includes bibliographical references.
Identifiers: LCCN 2018001103 (print) | LCCN 2018006164 (ebook) | ISBN
    9789004364486 (E-book) | ISBN 9789004364462 (pbk. : alk. paper) | ISBN
    9789004364479 (hardback : alk. paper)
Subjects: LCSH: Effective teaching. | Motivation in education.
Classification: LCC LB1025.3 (ebook) | LCC LB1025.3 .T537 2018 (print) | DDC
    371.102--dc23
LC record available at https://lccn.loc.gov/2018001103

Typeface for the Latin, Greek, and Cyrillic scripts: "Brill". See and download: brill.com/brill-typeface.

ISBN 978-90-04-36446-2 (paperback)
ISBN 978-90-04-36447-9 (hardback)
ISBN 978-90-04-36448-6 (e-book)

Contents

PART 2

What Does It Look Like? Responsive Dispositions in the Classroom

PART 3

Just Do It: Processes and Tools

Preface

Parents want their children to have good a teacher. Parents want their children to go to a good school. The question remains, "What is meant by good and how do we get there?" Good schools benefit not only individual children and their families but also our society as a whole. So, we all search for quality education. In the United States, this search is not new. We have had a Nation at Risk, the No Child Left Behind Act, Race to the Top and the Every Student Succeeds Act, all mandated in the name of quality education, but how do we measure education, and more specifically teacher quality? We look to standards for that answer.

Efforts are aimed at helping students to achieve at high levels of success. The determination of school effectiveness has rested soundly on standardized achievement test scores comparing child to child, school to school, district to district, state to state, and nation to nation. We award letter grades to indicate school quality, based on these tests. We know that the impact of a teacher on student learning is significant (Tucker & Stronge, 2005) and that the quality of the preparation of that teacher matters significantly when it comes to teacher effectiveness (Darling-Hammond, 2000). Thus, teacher preparation programs build on and respond to accreditation standards that provide descriptions of expectations for teachers' practices and professionalism, and states employ standards for teaching practices and licensure.

We search for quality teachers. By most definitions, a highly qualified teacher possesses content area knowledge, typically measured by counting content course hours taken in college and continuing education units accumulated through professional development such as workshops or conferences. Teacher effectiveness and quality have been linked to increased student test scores and value added measures; however, the concept of teacher quality is not so easily quantified. The limitations of these approaches to teacher quality and effectiveness are evident, but they yield desired data and numbers to "objectively "rank and reward teachers.

But there is something more to being a great teacher. Content understanding and teaching skills are necessary to teacher quality, but are they sufficient? Beyond the numbers, a closer examination of teaching and learning within our schools may reveal seemingly less tangible, yet significant factors that affect and indicate the quality of student learning that numbers cannot capture. Specifically, who a teacher is and what a teacher does in the classroom directly affects not only the daily lives of students but also their future lives as educated, democratic, 21st-century adults.

This book explores this somewhat less tangible teacher quality indicator called teacher dispositions. Dispositions have been part of teaching standards for several decades. Further, disposition evaluation tools are used throughout teacher preparation programs across the nation. The acknowledgment of the importance of who the teacher is as a person, beyond possessing needed knowledge and skill sets, is clear. Perhaps what is less clear is "What does that mean?" This book poses and discusses multiple questions related to teacher quality and teacher dispositions. The first section seeks to build a foundational understanding of the concept of dispositions and offers a construct, namely *Dispositions in Action*, to examine how teacher dispositions affect student learning. The second section is comprised of teachers' stories explaining and exemplifying *Dispositions in Action* in their real classrooms. Lastly, tools and approaches to evaluate *Dispositions in Action* are included, as well as suggestions for how they may be helpful to teachers, administrators, and everyday people to better understand and think about what we mean by and how we acquire quality teachers in our classrooms.

We have all had, or at least deserved to have a great teacher. These are the teachers who influence us as people, both as students in their classrooms and the adults we become. What is it that makes some teachers so good? What do they have that other teachers, even those who are smart and skilled at teaching, do not have? They have the *It factor*, the dispositions that set these teachers apart from others. This book asks, "What are teacher dispositions?" It examines what teacher dispositions look like in the classroom, in action. It explains why teachers with certain dispositions work better with students as learners. It also explores why dispositions matter, especially now.

A teacher's dispositions directly affect the kind of learning that takes place with students. Dispositions establish the framework and foundation for relationships within the classroom. They reveal how aspects of teaching and learning come to life. Dispositions affect the development of students as thinkers, collaborators, creators and decision-makers. Who a teacher is, how she or he is disposed to view, interpret, and determine what happens in the classroom, directly impacts students, and thus perhaps our future. This book allows us to think about, talk about, and use a definition of teacher dispositions that matters to student learning and the development of future leaders.

References

Darling-Hammond, L. (2000). Teacher quality and student achievement. *Education Policy Analysis Archives, 8*(1). Retrieved from https://doi.org/10.14507/epaa.v8n1.2000

Tucker, P. D., & Stronge, J. H. (2005). *Linking teacher evaluation and student learning*. Alexandria, VA: Association for Supervision and Curriculum Development.

PART 1

What Is It *and Why Does* It *Matter?*

..

CHAPTER 1

My Journey with Dispositions

Think about:

1 If students could change one thing about their learning experiences, what would it be?
2 Who and what affects how learning happens in the classroom?
3 What three words would you use to describe yourself (or someone you know) as a teacher?

• • •

I have spent the majority of my career as a professional educator trying to figure out what makes a good teacher. Perhaps what I was really wondering was, why aren't all teachers great? I knew from my own experiences as a student that some teachers were indeed better than others. I think seeing the differences between teachers and knowing how they made me feel as a learner was part of my motivation to become a teacher. When I finally got my own classroom, I was concerned about what my principal thought of my teaching, but mostly I was concerned about what my students thought and doing what was right by them. So, I did what I thought was right behind closed doors. I assumed that everybody else was pretty much doing the same thing. We were all trying to inspire our students. We were all challenging them and helping them reach their highest potential. We were teaching content for understanding and application to the real world, weaving concepts and experiences together so students could see the big picture and purpose of learning. Just as important as learning deeply, we wanted our students to love learning and choose to become lifelong learners.

It didn't take long for my assumption that teachers were all in it for the same reasons to be challenged. It started with my students. Every day in my classroom wasn't exciting and certainly not perfect. My skills as a teacher were not unique or extraordinary. But I did notice that students liked being in my classroom. Most days, they were actually excited about learning. The excitement and ownership fostered as I used reading and writing workshops was contagious. When things were going well in my classroom, my students would start to complain when it was time to switch classes and sometimes complain about the other teachers. They would ask, "Why can't Mrs. Smith let us choose what we want to read?" "That class is boring; why can't we do things

© KONINKLIJKE BRILL NV, LEIDEN, 2018 | DOI 10.1163/9789004364486_001

that are interesting?" "Can you tell them how we do group projects in here?" What happened in our classroom just felt different from their other classes, and they wanted me to help them fix it.

Then there were my principals. My first principal seemed a bit distant and busy, focused on keeping the school running smoothly and parents happy. My teaching evaluations were good and everything was fine. Things just kind of went the same day after day. My second principal spent a great deal more time with his teachers and really focused on "students first." Evaluations forms were only the starting point for in-depth discussions about teaching and learning and acting as professional educators. He was always seeking the why behind decisions, always with the student at the center and encouraging us to question conventions and assumptions. I enjoyed the push and the challenges and seemingly constant state of change. But not everyone else did. My desire to jump in the deep end and give things a try was not the norm. In fact, in many ways much of what I did as a teacher was different from most of my colleagues. But my principal valued it and I trusted him explicitly. I started to wonder not only how, but why differences in teachers existed. He inspired me to take on the challenge of learning how to be a better teacher not only for myself but also to try to make a contribution to my profession as a whole. I wanted to find out what we all needed to know and do to become great teachers.

I started by asking what made students and principals consider some teachers better than others. Why did some teachers take the risks of innovation to meet students' needs, the road less traveled, while others remained on the trodden down path year in and year out? In any case, I felt I owed it to my students to figure out how to help all of their teachers, including me, be good ones. I decided to enter and study the field of teacher preparation and professional development to find opportunities in my coursework and within my research to figure it out.

1   What Do Students Think about Teaching and Learning?

Since students had been the impetus for me to question what makes good teaching, I decided to use their thoughts and experiences as a starting point. First, I looked at the ways that students were experiencing teaching and learning in their classrooms. Our teaching team had been committed to using student-centered, developmentally responsive practices with young adolescent learners (Cook, Faulkner, & Howell, 2016). As a team, we had been attending professional conferences and engaging in professional reading and inquiry to try to develop the best educational experience for our students. Concepts such as James Beane's (1990) student driven curriculum and the use of outcomes-based education largely guided our curricular and instructional design. We determined curricular themes and co-designed instructional strategies with our students, addressing their questions about the world and guiding them to discover the answers. Themes such as conflict, the environment, and the universe became the focus of our learning as we built upon students' interests and concerns. We designed engaging learning experiences and used differentiation to work to meet all students' needs. The focus was on questioning, critiquing, analyzing, and understanding. Instead of content coverage driving instruction, content was the vehicle to engage students in these thought processes. Assessments were authentic and often collaborative in nature. Students developed and used reflective portfolios to demonstrate their learning and set learning goals for themselves. They discussed, with parents and guardians in student led conferences, how they had met goals and set future ones through sharing and explaining related work sample evidence. We used flexible schedules, flexible grouping, and various means of co-teaching between and among the regular classroom teachers and with our special education expert. Learning was dynamic and goals were set high. We lived the mantra "all students can learn."

When I asked my students to help me understand what they considered good teaching, I wasn't surprised that they often referred to many of the learning practices and structures we used on our team. Student driven curriculum gave them a sense of ownership and voice. Engaged, cooperative learning made school interesting, fun, and meaningful. Authentic assessment allowed students to show their strengths and understandings in multiple ways. They could make connections to the real world they lived in now and the future they hoped to create. I was excited to investigate what the students thought of this "new world" of school. We were using new approaches to curriculum, instruction and assessment. We had changed the very definition of schooling, but how did they view all of this? I wanted to know how they made sense of our thematic instruction and find out what strategies and assessments were the most valuable to them as learners. But when I asked about what helped them the most to be successful and happy in school, they went in a different direction. Our conversations about curriculum, assessment, student voice, and engaged learning faded into the background. Suddenly it was all about the teacher.

2   What Do Students Think about Teachers?

These conversations about what students thought about our "reformed" pedagogy morphed into a yearlong study where I delved into research for my impending dissertation. It was focused on students' perceptions of educational change and reform. As a researcher, I decided to learn with and from my middle schoolers. Observations, student work samples, and individual interviews made up the substance of the data I gathered. Some of the most intriguing parts of data collection came from the focus group interviews, where the students could share their own thoughts and exchange and build upon their ideas together. I continued to prompt them to dig deeper to articulate their thoughts and views on teaching and learning. It was during these conversations that I noticed the use of terms referring to teacher quality. Over their years of schooling they shared that they had encountered primarily four types of teachers. They said you could tell which type a teacher was by listening to and watching how the teacher talked and interacted with students. They spoke about the mean teacher, the nice teacher, the good teacher and then some different kind of teacher that was really good and nice. I wanted to know more and began conducting further study.

The methodology of this study included group interviews of students and individual histories of each student as a learner. The design was iterative and included multiple member checks for the student participants to help engage in forming conceptual understanding, as identified themes were shared with them and they elaborated on the ongoing findings. The initial group interviews focused on what really mattered to students who had experiences in traditional classrooms over multiple years, and now found themselves plunked into the middle of a progressive, student-centered teaching team. Emergent themes of teacher role, power, and relationships framed ongoing questions and analysis of individual learner histories. Themes generated from the individual histories were then recycled back through member checks. The next layer of themes became more precise and focused on two primary areas, namely classroom talk (or discourse) and the roles teachers and students chose to play. The student participants were also involved in helping to write up the initial findings, making sure that their words and ideas were evident throughout. The last step was the finalization of a conceptual map of the study results that detailed what happens at the intersection of discourse and roles in the classroom.

Although these students had recently been in "reformed" classrooms focused on student-centered, engaged, problem-based instruction, coupled with student-driven, integrated curriculum, that was not what mattered the most to them. Students knew what mattered the most was inside the teacher. The people teachers truly were determined how teachers acted and defined learning. The shared philosophy, pedagogies, and commitment to meeting students' needs were filtered through the teacher. They came to life through the teacher's interaction with the students and you could see and hear it.

The students' words were used to define emergent themes. The themes included relationship issues, or *"how teachers treat you,"* role expectations, *"how teachers and students act,"* and the way this affects learning through *"how you talk in the classroom."* They believed that talk was used to negotiate learning. According to the students, there were unwritten rules about talking in the classroom.

– Mostly teachers talk. Students take turns and only talk when called on.
– Talk must stick to the point.
– Talk is usually boring – same thing again and again.
– The teacher tells you stuff and what to do. Kids either listen or tune out.
– There is often controlling talk, such scolding or commands.
– Kids are supposed to tell the right answer and get it right the first time.
– No socializing is allowed. Kids can talk quietly if you are done with your "work."
– Don't ask too many questions.
– Teachers can "set you up" to look foolish with their questions.
– Answering when you are in trouble or explaining your actions is seen as talking back.
– Kids have no opinions.
– What a teacher says and does is based on the teacher's mood.

3   Talk as Functions of Discourse

The function of discourse in some classrooms was to *silence and control*. This occurred in impersonal classrooms where students and teachers played out their roles, focused on compliance, covering content, and completing work.

"If you give your opinion teachers think you are talking back. You can't disagree with what they are teaching; you can't explain when they ask what you are doing or when they yell at you. If you say anything; it's automatically disrespectful, even if you are sticking up for what you think is right. If you say what you think about something, you pay for it."

Teachers talked, students didn't. Student talking was viewed as bad and was punished. Asking questions was a sign of not listening or paying attention, or a challenge to the teacher's authority. Teacher talk was about academic content and how to do assignments. It was formal in the sense that it was devoid of personal feelings, or personal meanings. It was used to give directions, to praise and to reprimand. It was a privilege reserved for the teacher, but could be accessed by students when called upon to answer questions or share information (Thornton, 1996).

Some classroom discourse did include personal talk among students and teachers, but this happened outside of the learning process, at the classroom door in the morning, at recess or lunch, or as a break from work time. The predominant mode of talk in the classroom was a teacher monologue focused on content and skills, but on the side, once in a while, the talk could become more personal. The teacher might talk about her life outside of the classroom including her family, pets, and hobbies. Students could do the same, but not during a lesson.

There were some teachers who could intertwine personal talk and learning experiences which made learning more relevant and enjoyable for the students. People and learning were not separated. Learning was about developing individuals' theories, conceptions, and opinions while exploring content to develop an understanding of the people and the world around them. This was the discourse of real learning. This is what the students in the study valued the most.

4   Teacher Types

Students used discourse and interaction within the classroom to identify various teacher types: the mean teacher, the nice teacher, the good teacher and the special teacher.

The *mean teacher* was at the lowest end of teacher quality according to the students. This teacher's classroom was a place of extremes. At times students would not understand boundaries or intentionally cross them. This would lead to chaos and often intentional disruption of learning by some students, followed by frustration of others. This teacher just went through the motions trying to get to the end of the day. The goal was to cover material, get students to turn their work in and give out grades without too much interruption. Using good grades as a reward along with punishment of misbehavior helped things to go the way the teacher wanted. Almost all classroom talk was one way, teacher to students. Relationships were dangerous to this teacher. There was a very clear line between teacher and student and everyone was expected to conform to the norms of their roles and focus on self-control. This teacher's method of establishing relationships with students was typically one of telling, yelling, complaining, or just giving up. According to the students, nobody really liked to be in that classroom and very little learning went on. Being in this classroom was a matter of *survival*.

If the theme in the mean teacher's classroom was survival, the *nice teacher* was all about *acceptance*. This teacher had a positive attitude and would often greet students at the door with a big smile and a high five. She was friendly and liked to talk about life outside of school. She seemed real. Rewards were still external and typically comprised of grades, praise, free time and sometimes candy. The flow of information still went from teacher to student. Students were encouraged to take a guess at answers and typically were rewarded with a "good job," whether or not the answer was correct or even close. She was a teacher who would give extra credit to help raise your grades or would grade assignments more on effort than competency. Nevertheless, students really didn't feel like they were learning that much content in this classroom. At times, some people would take advantage of her kindness, leaving the other students to defend their beloved teacher and generally get the class back on track. They liked her; they just weren't sure what they were really learning. The A students did fine, everybody else got good grades for trying, but the nice teacher wasn't much better quality-wise than the mean teacher, if you looked at teaching and learning.

Then there was the *good* teacher. She also knew her stuff and had high expectations for learning. Her classes focused on *understanding*. This teacher listened to what students said and asked, gave them feedback and support, and guided them to finding the right answers. Lessons and concepts were clearly explained and help was readily given. But there was no monkey business. Teacher and student roles were clear and focused on academic success. Students behaved. Time was too precious to waste on anything other than learning, and learning was connected to success in the real world beyond school. Talk was centered on helping each other to find answers. In this classroom learning was valued and everyone worked together to achieve success.

Occasionally, some of the students had encountered a *special* teacher. This teacher was not only nice but she was good at helping students learn. Role expectations and related behaviors were not important. Teachers and students could be themselves and learning was about exploring and answering their own questions about the world. Learning became intrinsically enjoyable through engagement, ownership, and collaboration. Students' experiences were shared and valued within the learning process as the teacher made connections between content understanding and their lives. Talk was encouraged. In fact, talk was necessary as individuals worked, talked, and made sense of things together. The motivation to learn became increasingly intrinsic and there was less reliance on external motivation. This virtually eliminated the use of or need for control and punishment talk. Instead, talk about behavior centered on refocusing students on learning and encouraging students to take ownership of their actions and solve problems together. This classroom was about discovering who you could be and all that you could do. Being smart was cool.

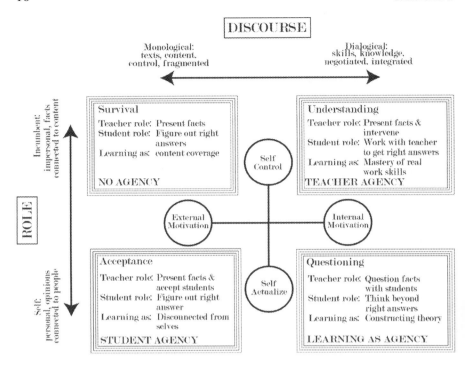

FIGURE 1.1   *Pedagogy: The intersection of discourse and role (from Thornton, 1996, reprinted with permission).*

5   What Role Do Structure and Power Play?

As I continued my journey as a professional educator, I found myself teaching at the university level and working with a cadre of strong, passionate, and competent teachers. I had the opportunity to work with them while supervising my students in the field and had several as students in my master's level courses. They were able to articulate and advocate for multiple best practices and research verified approaches, but for some reason they didn't seem to utilize them much in their classrooms. It seemed the vast majority of teachers with whom I worked wanted to be innovative, passionate, and highly effective educators. There had to be something holding them back. Was it a mandated curriculum? Was it expectations from school administrators or a lack of acknowledging the teacher's voice as decision-maker in the classroom? I decided to find out drawing on my research base and my teaching experiences with my previous teaching team of reformers.

Looking back, my team had engaged in professional development, reading, and collaborative inquiry, we discovered theory and practice that matched our shared philosophies and seemed to be just waiting for implementation.

We decided to develop and implement James Beane's (1990) concept of student driven curriculum coupled with the current trend of outcomes based education (Spady, 1994). Our principal empowered us to make decisions about designing curriculum and exploring authentic assessments, even to the point of developing an outcomes-based performance report card that did not use letter grades; but instead was grounded in a mastery and rework concept using "grades" of proficient and in progress. We ran with it. I documented how successful it was in terms of meaningful student learning and depth of understanding using work sample evaluation.

After four years of that reformed reality, I learned that my principal would be leaving our school. I could not imagine our work continuing without him. I decided to find another venue to continue my learning and research agenda. I soon found myself working as an associate professor in teacher preparation. I had the opportunity to work with strong teachers spread across multiple districts. They all wanted to implement what they knew was best for students drawing on their experiences and knowledge bases, which had an underlying middle school philosophy. I had lived a different, reformed life as a teacher and they were ready and wanted to do so too. I realized that the teachers weren't the challenge to reform and decided that it must be the structure and organization of their schools and the systems within which they worked. Structures limited their power and voice.

I spent three years cultivating relationships with these teachers within a professional development school model of teacher preparation. We had been talking, working, and thinking together about how to improve teaching and learning, specifically of at-risk students at the middle level. Collectively, we decided that we wanted to conceptualize and implement a model middle school, using research-verified practices that represented the student centered and responsive philosophy to which we were all committed. Thus, the summer academy was born. Substantial time was spent discussing philosophy, best practices, and developing a shared vision for the school that would take place with at-risk students (summer school assigned) from their own classrooms during the summer. It was a chance to implement all of this without the barriers embedded in the teachers' home schools. Collectively we created interdisciplinary student-driven curriculum, authentic performance-based assessments, and engaged problem-based learning opportunities. We were building a learning community to give all participants, especially students, a voice in the learning process and ownership in the school itself. Teachers were empowered. They called the shots. We built our school around their beliefs and expertise. Instead of having a principal or administrator, teachers contributed their strengths to accomplish needed tasks. Everyone worked together in whatever capacity made sense, blurring the roles and boundaries, all with a focus on learning. The teachers were excited. The kids were excited. It was utopia.

But not really. Acting as the researcher for our collaborative work, I would document successes and areas in need of improvement. I collected data through student and teacher interviews, classroom observations, and student learning performances and work samples. I used the SOLO taxonomy (Biggs & Collis, 2014) to evaluate depth of understanding within the student artifacts. It did not take long to notice an emergent trend. In multiple classrooms, students and teachers were flourishing and philosophy and practice became one. However, that was not the case in every classroom. Teachers had free rein to act as decision-makers in the classroom and school. But, even on the same teaching teams, there was a noticeable difference in the way teachers lived and enacted this shared vision. Weren't the structural changes to remove barriers and ownership to empower teachers to live their philosophy enough? Some classrooms were exemplars of what we had been trying to achieve in terms of teaching and learning. Others were merely modifications of traditional practices. There was something about the teachers who flourished in this culture that was different from those who did not. What was it?

6   Dispositions

It seemed the difference was something internal. Something other than pedagogical knowledge and content expertise. Something beyond sound classroom management and engaged learning. All of the teachers were using student-driven curriculum, engaged, problem-based learning and other best practices. It was all grounded in the shared development of the academy's vision and mission. Even so, there were significant differences in teaching and learning within our academy, and within the way teachers enacted these approaches to teaching. Why? I began to explore the concept of educator dispositions.

This exploration eventually lead me to the development of the concept of *Dispositions in Action*. As I continued to explore the literature related to educator dispositions, I found that direct evidence of how these dispositions impact student learning remained missing participatory research with master teachers and their preservice teacher partners helped me to continue my quest to understand teacher dispositions better. The *Dispositions in Action* construct continued to be developed and refined across several years, many school contexts, and multiple studies. *Dispositions in Action* analyzes classroom interaction to reveal teacher dispositions through the examination of classroom relationships and patterns of talk and dialogue. Ultimately, there are two categories of educator dispositions within this model: responsive and technical. They are evidenced in teacher interactions within the domains of management, assessment, instruction, and professional behavior. Teachers who evidence responsive dispositions are committed to student empowerment, critical thinking, and facilitative learning. Those evidencing technical dispositions are more concerned with issues of compliance and finding the correct answer, as they use teacher centered approaches. Responsive dispositions seemed clearly aligned with goals for effective teaching and multiple standard sets. They echoed and supported much of the literature about quality teaching. Now that I had discovered this and identified these orientations towards educator dispositions, it was time to figure out what to do about it.

Think again:

1 What kind of teacher is typically found in classrooms (from your experience) mean, nice, good or special? Why do you think that is so? Can it or should it change?
2 How valid and reliable is using students' perceptions/voice to inform educational change? When and how should student voice be used in instructional decisions?
3 Have you ever engaged in a "reform" effort? What were the results? Why do you think things turned out that way?
4 How do you define teacher dispositions? Do you have experience with the evaluation of dispositions?

References

Beane, J. A. (1990). *A middle school curriculum: From rhetoric to reality.* Westerville, OH: NMSA.

Biggs, J. B., & Collis, K. F. (2014). *Evaluating the quality of learning: The SOLO taxonomy (structure of the observed learning outcome).* New York, NY: Academic Press.

Cook, C. M., Faulkner, S. A., & Howell, P. B. (2016). The developmentally responsive middle school: Meeting the needs of all students. *Middle School Journal, 47*(5), 3–13.

Spady, W. (1994). *Outcome-based education: Critical issues and answers.* Arlington, VA: American Association of School Administrators.

Thornton, H. J. (1996). *Kids' voices in educational reform research: What really matters, the social negotiation of role and discourse as definers of pedagogy* (Doctoral dissertation). The Ohio State University, Columbus, OH.

CHAPTER 2

Dispositions in Action: What Do They Look Like?

Think about:

1 What kind of decisions do teachers make on a daily basis?
2 What do you think influences those decisions?
3 What is your understanding of *Dispositions in Action* so far?

• • •

If dispositions are foundational to good teaching, we need to find a means to examine them within the current context and challenges of being a teacher. We need more than labels and definitions for teacher dispositions. We need to understand what these dispositions mean. What do they look like in practice and how do we know what dispositions a teacher has? If we can build a shared understanding of what DIA, *Dispositions in Action*, and more specifically responsive dispositions, look like in comparison to technical dispositions, we can further understand and explore what dispositions mean to student learning.

High stakes testing leads to a definition of learning where teachers adopt strategies that lead to test score gains. The focus is on a technical "how to" version of teaching as multiple benchmark and practice tests are given and curriculum guides are carefully followed. This perpetuates the belief that educator competence is defined by professional knowledge and skills, and that alone is sufficient for producing teacher excellence (Collinson, 1999). But there is more to teaching and teachers than technical skills and content knowledge. Real teaching is not a scripted performance, but rather it consists of a myriad of decisions teachers make minute by minute that weave together the interactions and relationships that define learning and teaching. Underlying, all of these pedagogical decisions are foundational dispositions. Dispositions are what animates, motivates, and directs teachers' abilities. They are visibly present in patterns of frequently exhibited behavior, or actions (Ritchhart, 2001). In order to begin to understand how dispositions affect teaching, we need to have a lens through which to view them in the life of the classroom, where impactful decisions are made. This is where *Dispositions in Action* (DIA) come into play. *Dispositions in Action* help us to answer the question, "If teachers have certain dispositions, then what does that mean for learning?"

Dispositions in Action provide a framework that allows us to examine how teacher dispositions affect teaching and learning, what they "look like" in practice. Rather than focusing on prevalent approaches to teacher dispositions in the field such as using professional behavior checklists, self-reflective journaling, hypothetical case analyses, or setting up a data system to document standards evaluation for accreditation, DIA examines how dispositions are manifested in the classroom setting through teacher/student interactions (Thornton, 2006). *Dispositions in Action* reflect two emergent categories of dispositions: responsive and technical (Thornton, 2006).

Given the current context and challenges of schooling, it may not be surprising that we are able to find teachers who are technically disposed. The concept of teacher as technician is related to other technical fields such as management science, computer science, and operations research. A technical approach is well-defined, traceable, and intentionally structured using systems-based thinking. When one is disposed to think technically about teaching and learning there is reliance systems, such as a fixed curriculum, school wide discipline policy and pacing guides. The teacher is disposed to be methodical in procedure, logical, efficient, and thorough. Technicians are inclined to have scripts that they follow. There is often little variation from situation to situation and student to student. If they identify a problem or situation they look to someone, an expert or decision-maker, who knows what to do and can provide explicit steps that tell them how to proceed. Everything depends on accuracy and precision. Teachers who are technically disposed know how to employ the skills of teaching successfully, but are not highly valued for examining the "why" behind instructional decisions. Instead, learning is about efficiency and accountability.

Responsively disposed teachers not only understand the need for specific procedures, they are inclined to respond to what happens in the learning process and thoughtfully react. They know how to interpret results, make decisions based on what they find, and know how to explain what is happening in their classrooms in terms of research support and theoretical grounding. The responsive disposition is a thinking-based orientation that is responsive in many dimensions: responsive to the needs and actions of the learner, their developmental characteristics, understanding, student questions, student work, and the learning context. They do not just act; they respond, making multiple decisions and changes. A responsive disposition by nature is necessarily fluid and changing. Responsive teachers understand the generative nature of learning, as new conceptions are discovered and new paths created with students, always pushing ahead and moving beyond traditional barriers.

Teachers possess either responsive or technical dispositions. It is not a clear-cut dichotomy or an either or, but rather can be thought of as a continuum between one orientation towards thinking, or habit of mind, and another.

A teacher's dispositions may be evidenced differently when related to what is transpiring in the classroom. Evidence of DIA can be aligned with major classroom functions, or domains, where they are typically exhibited. These domains of practice include instruction, assessment, management and professionalism as described in Table 2.1 below.

TABLE 2.1   *Dispositions in Action (Thornton, 2006).*

Responsive	Domain	Technical
The disposition to be *Critical* in one's thinking. Evidenced in dialogue that is: probing, focused on quality, centered on criteria, concerned with deep understanding	Assessment	The disposition to be *Assuming* in one's thinking. Evidenced in dialogue that is: centered on completion of tasks, focused on correctness, concerned with grades
The disposition to be *Challenging* in one's thinking. Evidenced in dialogue that is: centered on high expectations, student competence and success for all students		The disposition to be *Accepting* in one's thinking. Evidenced in dialogue that is: indicative of low expectations, focused on effort and compliance
The disposition to be *Facilitative* in one's thinking. Evidenced in dialogue that is: guiding, inquiry oriented, concerned with application and connections to students' lives, and real world examples, in search of multiple answers and the exchange of ideas	Instruction	The disposition to be *Directing* in one's thinking. Evidenced in dialogue that is: about directing actions of students, coverage of facts, telling information and giving answers
The disposition to be *Creative* in one's thinking. Evidenced in dialogue that is: about multiple ways of framing learning, examples, and paths to understanding diverse learners, responsive to students' questions, comments		The disposition to be *Repetitive* in one's thinking. Evidenced in dialogue that is: lacking in variety in explaining, exemplifying or representing learning, repetitive, the same way for all students

Responsive	Domain	Technical
The disposition to be *Empowering* in one's thinking. Evidenced in dialogue that is: concerned with student input related to classroom instructional decisions, centered on fairness and equity		The disposition to be *Controlling* in one's thinking. Evidenced in dialogue that is: concerned with managing student behaviors and actions including movement, talking, and other forms of interaction
	Management	
The disposition to be in *Connected* one's thinking. Evidenced in dialogue that is: centered on developmental needs, exhibits "withitness" problem solving, conflict resolution and responsiveness to students as individuals		The disposition to be *Distanced* in one's thinking. Evidenced in dialogue that is: often limited, general in nature, generic, often remaining the same from class to class and situation to situation
The disposition to be *Change-driven* in one's thinking. Evidenced in dialogue that is: concerned with improvement of education as a whole, focused on research-based action, indicative of continuous professional growth for self and others, willing to question those in power.		The disposition to be *Compliance-driven* in one's thinking. Evidenced in dialogue that is: concerned with following mandates and directives, focused on not disrupting the status quo or calling unnecessary attention to oneself or one's school, wanting to please, appease those in power, reward driven.
	Professionalism	
The disposition to be *Inclusive* in one's thinking. Evidenced in dialogue that is: representative of multiple perspectives, concerned with giving voice to others, seeking collaboration, reciprocity and ownership, and leadership from all stakeholders		The disposition to be *Hierarchical* in one's thinking. Evidenced in dialogue that is: limited in terms of voice and power, seeking approval of authority, using authority over others, role-oriented

DIA are also found within professional interactions with colleagues, administrators, and the community. In this domain, responsive teachers are change driven, seeking continuous improvement and innovation, and inclusive, building upon collaboration with others and valuing voice for all. In contrast, technical teachers are hierarchical and compliant. Their professional behaviors are grounded in carrying out the decisions of those "higher up" such as school boards, superintendents, principals, and department chairs. Their actions and interactions are focused on professional accountability and following policies, guidelines, and school-based mores.

In many ways student learning is defined by the teacher's *Dispositions in Action*. A teacher's dispositions frame the teacher's perception of events that occur and the resulting instructional decisions. In classrooms where teachers exhibit responsive dispositions, student learning is focused on deeper understanding, where students are encouraged to ask questions, examine assumptions, and construct new meanings. Whereas, teachers who exhibit technical dispositions have classrooms where students are encouraged to seek and remember correct answers in an efficient, straightforward manner.

The impact of dispositions on teaching and learning may be significant over the years. Studies indicate that it is likely that the *Dispositions in Action* pre-service teachers demonstrate at the end of their preparation program remain relatively constant and unchanged as they enter their beginning years as professional educators (Thornton, 2013). Although teachers' *Dispositions in Action* remained constant over time, they were not necessarily correlated with different school contexts or the content areas being taught. Even though there were differences in these novice teachers' schools, many characteristics were the same. All were dealing with a strong emphasis on standardized high-stakes testing via No Child Left Behind mandates. All were held accountable to these tests and were successful in getting students to do well on them. However, the young teachers' dispositions affected how they reacted to the testing focus and how they ultimately enacted teaching and created learning in their classrooms (Thornton, 2013).

So let's meet these two types of teachers. Those who are technically disposed fall into step with standardized professional expectations and tend to be successful with implementing the type of learning whose end goal is to raise test scores. In their classrooms, content coverage and student compliance lead to productive learning. On the other hand, those that are responsively disposed focus on practices that emphasize teaching for understanding, critical thinking, and student decision making. Students believe that their learning experiences with responsive teachers were more positive overall than their experiences with technical ones. The vignettes that follow help us to think about the classroom-based meaning of DIA.

1   **Assessment as Defining Expectations**

1.1   *Evidence of a Technical Disposition*

Jarrad and Dante finish up with their presentation. Their project is clearly missing some of the criteria of the rubric; a rubric that had been passed out to them to guide the assignment's completion, but had not since been discussed with students as to meaning ... but students can always ask the teacher. All of the required project elements are found in their presentation. They have the data sources, the questions, the findings, the connections to their community in the past and now. However, it is not clear that the pair understood all of the terms they used, or grounded their findings in any type of framework or conceptual thinking. Connections are not clearly made between the data and the community, and they did not share the mathematical processes of statistical analysis that lead them to arrive at their conclusions. Some misconceptions are evident in their conclusions and use of the data. They had gone through the rubric, like a checklist, did and said what they were required to and were now "done."

They stand before the class, as students sit quietly watching and listening (or not) awaiting the teacher's response to the presentation. The teacher, who had been recording points on the rubric as the students presented, looks up and speaks. "Good work! Any questions?" Some students ask what part did Jarrad and Dante like the best, and if they got to talk to the judge when they went downtown to the courthouse to do some of their research. Dante says, "Yeah, the judge was pretty cool. But you don't want to mess with him." The teacher responds, "I bet ..." and then looks around, smiles and says, "Next group? Now everyone make sure to write down three new facts you learned in your journal to turn in for a grade at the end of the day." And the presentations continue.

1.2   *Evidence of a Responsive Disposition*

Chantal and Robert take the lead in sharing the data analysis of their research. They respond to the teacher's and other students' questions about why they made certain choices in their work, how they came to results and conclusions, and then share the processes they went through as they made design decisions. They also discuss the challenges they had to address and revisions they had to make. Helping to design the rubric, with the teacher, and using it as a reference during multiple conferences with the her and peers while working on their project and presentation, made the students feel comfortable with it as they used it to help them make sense of their work.

As Robert reveals the statistical analysis of the data on crime in the nation, in comparison to their city, the teacher interjects, "Why do you think those differences exist?" which leads to discussions by the pair. Other members of the class chime in.

"I noticed that you decided that more black males are convicted of crimes because of prejudice ... are there other factors that could contribute to that statistic as well? How did you incorporate these? As a follow up, why don't you look into the poverty and literacy issues you just shared and tie them back into your project ..and then I can take another look at it?"

As the pair finishes sharing, the teacher asks, "What were the strengths of Robert and Chantel's presentation?" Students look at their notes about the presentation they had added to their "State of Our City" journals and share feedback with the pair.

"What were some things they could change now, or consider next time to make their case even stronger?" Students ask questions and make suggestions based on the rubric criteria. Later, the teacher makes comments to challenge some of the group's assertions. The teacher guides this discussion and redirects it, bringing the whole class into the mix. "Who agrees with Chantal's last point... thumbs up or down...who thinks Steven's conclusion in his presentation was more accurate... why? What can we learn from both points of view ... is there common ground?" She continues, "Make sure to ask each presentation pair the questions you still have in our State of the City blog by the end of class and they can consider them and reply. Also, remember to record the big ideas you got from the presentation and include factual evidence or opinions they provided to back it up."

2   Instruction as Interaction

2.1   *Evidence of a Technical Disposition*

After the class reads an article aloud about Carver High school, the teacher talks about how the media portrays conflict. Literary devices are listed on the board, students copy the definitions down, and the teacher tells them, "Later we will use these to write a news script for a newscast, so don't lose them. Put them into your yellow notebook and put today's date in the upper right hand corner. Get out the sheet from yesterday that says ... WHO, WHERE, WHEN, WHY and HOW on it. We will use this in the computer lab today." Later they go to the computer lab to look up examples of media coverage of major world conflicts. The teacher gives them a list of the conflicts and the URL for each website. "You need to get the main ideas from each of these stories and web pages because we will be making a newscast later. We only have 20 minutes so make sure you go to all of the websites and get all of the important information: who, where, when why and how." Students go to the computer lab and the teacher reminds them about plagiarism and not to copy things word for word, or it will affect their grades. Students cut and paste information from the websites onto a clipboard. They sit with raised hands, waiting for the teacher to give them more directions or rush ahead with the task to have time to surf the web while the teacher is elsewhere in the room. She periodically reminds them to work more quietly. They work at this for 30 minutes, then return to the classroom.

2.2   *Evidence of a Responsive Disposition*

The teacher begins the lesson by asking questions about yesterday's class and the students respond. He builds on their comments, and then uses questions to make connections to students' lives and the learning goals he developed with them earlier that day. "What did you think of the story about the gangs in Carver High School yesterday? Do you know anyone who goes to Carver? Was the story very realistic to you? Why or why not? What did the writer use to try to get your attention ... what were some of the literary devices we talked about in the magazines yesterday... did you see any in there? Could they have used some others...what was the author's purpose?"

"Let's take our notes from yesterday's work on the magazines, and the essential questions from our brainstormed list to the computer lab. We can use them to see if other stories on conflict in our city in the past are portrayed in the same way... and then take a look at some key news stories on conflict from the past. But, first what stories on conflict from our past do you know about already? Let's make a list you can use to help your get started on locating useful articles on the internet. You also might want to look at keywords you have added to the vocabulary section of your writing journal. They might be in other stories that could be related and useful."

As the students work in the lab, they pull up the guide sheet they generated yesterday in class, to help them get the main ideas from the articles they are researching. They cut and paste examples for their guide sheet, knowing that later they will pull the information together into their own concept map and then an outline for their world news story. The teacher circulates around the room, redirecting students, and reminds them to ask their research buddies if they have a question. Students use their key word lists and brainstorming from class to guide their work. The teacher stops to give the class tips. He shares what one student is doing as an example. Students work with their buddies and eagerly share websites and information with their peers and the teacher as they find them. The teacher reminds them to use credible sources and note their URLs. The students begin to plug new ideas into the concept map they have started, weaving the content from social studies and history into their focus on journalism and writing. "Ok, let's go back to the workroom, and set learning goals for tomorrow's class time, and see what questions we still have about the newscast."

3   Management as Relationships

3.1   *Evidence of a Technical Disposition*

"I need everyone's attention. We have a problem we need to take care of right now. We have a contract that you all came up with and now I need to remind you to follow it. It is all about respect, and someone is not respecting the learning of others. The college students down the hall can't learn because someone isn't being respectful of others." The teacher goes on to talk about how lucky the students are to have their summer academy on a real college campus and how the dean is going to get very upset if the students from the academy are too loud. They need to act like adults and follow adult rules if they are going to have the privilege of being on a campus. She calls a community meeting to solve the problem. "Here we are all responsible for following the rules. We can have no snack machine." (the students grumble) "Or we can follow the rules you set." The teacher leads a discussion where the students get a choice of consequences that will happen if they are caught being too loud at the snack machine, setting up a kind of strike system, eventually leading to a loss of snack privileges. They write this up as a new snack machine contract. They then discuss how the noise level will be monitored and set up a watch system to make sure the new rules are followed. "Now that we have all agreed, these are your rules, and if we can't be responsible citizens of our learning community, we might lose that privilege ... does everyone agree?" Students nod and class begins.

3.2   *Evidence of a Responsive Disposition*

"Okay, everyone has done a great job of making and keeping our contract for learning while we are here on campus. The students are living up to their end of the bargain, watching out for one another, helping each other learn, helping the teachers learn. We've been working out problems before they have happened except one small problem. It is happening before we start in the morning and it is disrupting others' learning."

"Uh, oh... it's the snack machines"

"Yes, so let's have a community meeting and figure this out... the college students we share the building with are trying to work and study and we are making too much noise... so what do we do?" The students brainstorm some ideas. Some say no snack machine. Others says some of them don't have any food at home in the morning and that's all they get to eat. Others suggest then students can take turns bringing in snacks for everybody. Another student says that maybe some people don't have money for that. Someone laughs. The teacher interjects, "If we are all here for each other like the contract you all came up with... and no put downs... let's not go there...let's work this out... bringing in food for a lot of people is expensive for all of us...so what can we do?"

"We could just be quiet in the hallway...then it won't be a problem"

The teacher adds, "But did we find another problem now?"

"Yeah, don't laugh at other people's money situation and being hungry." The students go on to find a solution to make sure they don't come to school hungry and decide to add hunger to their list of issues and problems in society.

Let us look at what we can learn from these vignettes. The two teacher types, responsive and technical, are both illustrated within the same domain and define that domain essentially the same way conceptually. In the assessment vignettes, both teachers use expectations to guide student work and their evaluation of that work. Both teachers in the second set of vignettes see support as essential to teaching their curriculum and making instructional choices. The next pair both consider relationships as the key to classroom management. However, the actions taken in their classrooms are very different. This is because dispositions act as a filter for teachers' knowledge, skills, and beliefs. The vignettes demonstrate how they directly influence the choices and actions one takes in the classroom. DIA come to life within relationships, as the teacher makes meaning with students to understand new concepts and ideas. Whether a technically disposed teacher creates learning opportunities that emphasize seeking correct answers through adherence to rules and procedures, or the responsively disposed teacher emphasizes learning that exhibits questioning through deeper understanding, both teachers can be successful in attaining the learning goals they are disposed to value.

Our education profession needs to articulate standards for dispositions that lead to the kind of teaching and learning we value the most. Responsively disposed teachers may feel like they are teaching against the grain at this time in education. The dispositions we choose to value and cultivate as part of our teacher preparation and professional development should reflect what we value in future teachers. Our decisions about teaching dispositions should be made because we believe that specific dispositions will best support the development of the kind of teachers who are best suited to teach and reach students and further the goals of our profession. Whether we seek new teachers who possess and exhibit these dispositions through screening processes at entry to preparation programs or we intentionally cultivate them through coursework and field experiences, it is certain that pre-service teachers do possess and exhibit a set of dispositions when they enter the field as beginning professionals and continue to make decisions as career professionals.

Think again:

1   Consider each pair of vignettes. What are the strengths each teacher in the pair evidence? What do the two teachers have in common in their classroom practices? How do they define the domain in similar ways? How are they different?
2   Which of the two teachers in each vignette can you relate to the most? Why? Do you believe you are more technical or responsive in your dispositions? How is this reflected in your instructional decisions? Can you give an example?
3   Is your disposition the same across each of the four domains: assessment, curriculum and instruction, management, professionalism? Why do you think you possess certain dispositions and make certain decisions in your classroom?

References

Collinson, V. (1999). Redefining teacher excellence. *Theory into Practice, 38*(1), 4–11.

Ritchhart, R. (2001). From IQ to IC: A dispositional view of intelligence. *Roeper Review, 23*(3), 143–150.

Thornton, H. (2006). Dispositions in action: Do dispositions make a difference in practice? *Teacher Education Quarterly, 33*(2), 53–68.

Thornton, H. (2013). A case analysis of middle level teacher preparation and long-term teacher dispositions. *Research in Middle Level Education, 37*(3), 1–19. Retrieved March 18, 2017, from http://www.amle.org/portals/0/pdf/rmle/rmle_vol37_no3.pdf

CHAPTER 3

What Are Dispositions, Really?

Think about:

1 How do you define teacher quality?
2 What frameworks or constructs have been helpful to you in defining and articulating teacher quality?
3 What remains unclear in your understanding of dispositions?

•••

By exploring how *Dispositions in Action* relate to the broader field of educator dispositions and we can get a clearer picture of how dispositions may be related to teacher quality. Learning more about educator dispositions as a field of study helped me to discover and understand the usefulness of *Dispositions in Action*. The holy trinity of teacher quality has been knowledge, skills, and dispositions over the last several decades. An attempt to quantify complex concepts such as depth of teachers' knowledge, proficiency of their pedagogical skills, and how they are disposed to think and act as educators has been going on in the name of accountability and to prove the value of teacher education. Tests of content knowledge such as Praxis II, observational skills checklists such as Danielson's Framework and other measures attempt to codify what we mean by quality teaching. The focus has been on determining and measuring content expertise and pedagogical prowess. There is a solid research base related to teacher content knowledge, pedagogical content knowledge, and evidencing best or research-verified practices. The tools and assessments used to evaluate those measures of teacher quality are considered to have validation and substance within the profession. Teaching standards describe teaching as a set of highly complex tasks. However, much of what currently passes for teacher evaluation follows a reductionist approach. There is temptation not to evaluate perhaps what is most important, but rather to evaluate what is easy to measure.

Dispositions pose further challenges. They are not easy to define, let alone measure. I have spent nearly 30 years as an educator investigating and chasing this illusive concept. Dispositional assessments tend to reflect reductionism, superficiality, disconnectedness, and a culture of compliance (Diez, 2006). Their complex, personal, ambiguous, and potentially controversial nature has influenced both the quantity and quality of research and emergent tools used

© KONINKLIJKE BRILL NV, LEIDEN, 2018 | DOI 10.1163/9789004364486_003

to evaluate educator dispositions. There are three primary means by which dispositions have been defined, and thus evaluated in recent years. These include CAEP/NCATE professional standards for teaching, self-reflection or response to specific scenarios, and observational checklists of behavior.

CAEP/NCATE does not provide discussion of any theoretical framework or sources for its model of dispositions. Further, there is little in its definition of dispositions to suggest that CAEP/NCATE has moved to a performance-based model (Freeman, 2003). Perhaps this is because, according to CAEP (2017), research has not empirically established a particular set of non-academic qualities that teachers should possess.

According to CAEP,

> There are numerous studies that list different characteristics, sometimes referring to similar characteristics by different labels. Furthermore, there does not seem to be a clear measure for these non-academic qualities, although a few of them have scales and other measures that have been developed. The CAEP Commission recognizes the ongoing development of this knowledge base and recommends that CAEP revise criteria as evidence emerges. The Commission recognizes the INTASC standards' set of dispositions as a promising area of research.

INTASC defines "critical dispositions" that indicate a teacher's moral commitments and habits of professional action which underlie teaching performance. These dispositions play a key role in teachers action within their classroom practice. These critical dispositions are aligned with each INTASC standards-based performance task in hopes of providing a means to evaluate related beliefs, attitudes, morals and ethics, and professional responsibilities. Terms such as committed, responsible, values, believes, respects and appreciates, are the verbs for the dispositional descriptors INTASC utilizes. This begs the question, how does one observe, let alone measure and evaluate such verbs? Portions of INTASC's dispositional descriptors begin to make connections to some teacher behaviors in the classroom. The majority of teacher preparation programs develop dispositional assessment measures that are grounded in the INTASC dispositional standards indicated below.

1   INTASC Standards

> Principle #1: The teacher understands the central concepts, tools of inquiry, and structures of the discipline(s) he or she teaches and can create learning experiences that make these aspects of subject matter meaningful for students.

Dispositions:

- The teacher *realizes* that subject matter knowledge is not a fixed body of facts but is complex and ever-evolving. S/he *seeks* to keep abreast of new ideas and understandings in the field.
- The teacher *appreciates* multiple perspectives and conveys to learners how knowledge is developed from the vantage point of the knower.
- The teacher has *enthusiasm* for the discipline(s) s/he teaches and *sees* connections to everyday life.
- The teacher is *committed* to continuous learning and engages in professional discourse about subject matter knowledge and children's learning of the discipline.

Principle #2: The teacher understands how children learn and develop, and can provide learning opportunities that support their intellectual, social and personal development

Dispositions:

- The teacher *appreciates* individual variation within each area of development, shows *respect* for the diverse talents of all learners, and is *committed* to help them develop self-confidence and competence.
- The teacher is disposed to use students' strengths as a basis for growth, and their errors as an opportunity for learning.

Principle #3: The teacher understands how students differ in their approaches to learning and creates instructional opportunities that are adapted to diverse learners students' learning is influenced by individual experiences, talents, and prior learning, as well as language, culture, family and community values.

Dispositions:

- The teacher *believes* that all children can learn at high levels and persists in helping all children achieve success.
- The teacher *appreciates* and *values* human diversity, shows *respect* for students' varied talents and perspectives, and is *committed* to the pursuit of "individually configured excellence."
- The teacher *respects* students as individuals with differing personal and family backgrounds and various skills, talents, and interests.
- The teacher is *sensitive* to community and cultural norms.
- The teacher makes students *feel valued* for their potential as people, and helps them learn to value each other.

Principle #4: The teacher understands and uses a variety of instructional strategies to encourage students' development of critical thinking, problem solving, and performance skills.

Dispositions:
- The teacher *values* the development of students' critical thinking, independent problem solving, and performance capabilities.
- The teacher *values* flexibility and reciprocity in the teaching process as necessary for adapting instruction to student responses, ideas, and needs.

Principle #5: The teacher uses an understanding of individual and group motivation and behavior to create a learning environment that encourages positive social interaction, active engagement in learning, and self motivation.

Dispositions:
- The teacher takes *responsibility* for establishing a positive climate in the classroom and participates in maintaining such a climate in the school as whole.
- The teacher *understands* how participation supports commitment, and is *committed* to the expression and use of democratic values in the classroom.
- The teacher *values* the role of students in promoting each other's learning and recognizes the importance of peer relationships in establishing a climate of learning.
- The teacher *recognizes* the value of intrinsic motivation to students' life-long growth and learning.
- The teacher is *committed* to the continuous development of individual students' abilities and *considers* how different motivational strategies are likely to encourage this development for each student.

Principle #6: The teacher uses knowledge of effective verbal, nonverbal, and media communication techniques to foster active inquiry, collaboration, and supportive interaction in the classroom.

Dispositions:
- The teacher *recognizes* the power of language for fostering self-expression, identity development, and learning.
- The teacher *values* many ways in which people seek to communicate and encourages many modes of communication in the classroom.

- The teacher is a *thoughtful* and responsive listener.
- The teacher *appreciates* the cultural dimensions of communication, responds appropriately, and seeks to foster culturally sensitive communication by and among all students in the class.

Principle #7: The teacher plans instruction based upon knowledge of subject matter, students, the community, and curriculum goals.

Dispositions:
- The teacher *values* both long term and short term planning.
- The teacher *believes* that plans must always be open to adjustment and revision based on student needs and changing circumstances.
- The teacher *values* planning as a collegial activity.

Principle #8: The teacher understands and uses formal and informal assessment strategies to evaluate and ensure the continuous intellectual, social and physical development of the learner.

Dispositions:
- The teacher *values* ongoing assessment as essential to the instructional process and *recognizes* that many different assessment strategies, accurately and systematically used, are necessary for monitoring and promoting student learning.
- The teacher is *committed* to using assessment to identify student strengths and promote student growth rather than to deny students access to learning opportunities.

Principle #9: The teacher is a reflective practitioner who continually evaluates the effects of his/her choices and actions on others (students, parents, and other professionals in the learning community) and who actively seeks out opportunities to grow professionally.

Dispositions:
- The teacher *values* critical thinking and self-directed learning as habits of mind.
- The teacher is *committed* to reflection, assessment, and learning as an ongoing process.
- The teacher is *willing* to give and receive help.
- The teacher is *committed* to seeking out, developing, and continually refining practices that address the individual needs of students.

- The teacher *recognizes* his/her professional responsibility for engaging in and supporting appropriate professional practices for self and colleagues.

Principle #10: The teacher fosters relationships with school colleagues, parents, and agencies in the larger community to support students' learning and well-being

Dispositions:
- The teacher *values* and *appreciates* the importance of all aspects of a child's experience. The teacher is *concerned* about all aspects of a child's well-being (cognitive, emotional, social, and physical), and is alert to signs of difficulties.
- The teacher is *willing* to consult with other adults regarding the education and wellbeing of his/her students.
- The teacher *respects* the privacy of students and confidentiality of information. The teacher is willing to work with other professionals to improve the overall learning environment for students.

Measuring dispositions based on a definition that focuses on moral commitments and professional habits is obviously problematic. Much research and literature about teacher dispositions speaks to the notion of dispositions as morals. Standard language may allude to the inclusion of moral development within disposition standards; however, there are multiple reasons why the majority of teacher preparation programs have not fully embraced equating dispositions with moral character. This is understandable given the ambiguity and complexity of evaluating the moral dimensions of teaching. There is a lack of ethical and moral language in teacher education curriculum and classrooms (Campbell, 2003) and little attention to ethical and moral dimensions of teaching (Sanger & Osguthorpe, 2011). When teacher education programs do address moral and ethical development theory and practice it is typically addressed in broad terms and assessed within candidate dispositions. This is often problematic according to Osguthorpe (2013) and typically results in a

cobbled together list of traits, values, beliefs, and attitudes ...derived from discussions of several faculty members who are sitting around a table, trying to achieve consensus on what is important, without any discussion of philosophical underpinnings—be they habits of mind, virtues, abilities, or some other logically coherent and sound concept. It is easy to recognize the value of theory and philosophical grounding when it comes to knowledge and skills, but too many of us rely on our intuitions and practical experience alone when it comes to dispositions. (p. 19)

The lack of theoretical grounding and consensus about dispositions may lead to the use of a technical approach, focusing on skills such as oral and written communication, class attendance, listening ability, and peer collaboration. This technical approach is typically grounded in the assumption that it is impossible to agree on anything related to morality; thus, consensus is sought in assessments that do not require any judgment of moral value (Wilkerson, 2006).

Seeking consensus in the evaluation of moral and ethical dimensions of teaching becomes controversial as questions arise regarding whose morals and ethics should be taught. The individualism and freedom of thought and speech within our democratic system exacerbates the differences between individuals' and groups' beliefs about what is moral. Concern about government intervention and dominance within a realm that is deemed personal, community-based and often religiously grounded is voiced. An "us" versus "them" mentality towards people who are different is perpetuated in media and politics. The diverse cultural nature of our society makes it difficult to define morality in ways that are universally agreeable. The National Council for Accreditation of Teacher Education came under fire for using the term "social justice" in reference to teacher dispositions. Supporters of a traditional curriculum have argued that evaluating students based on their commitment to social justice or other dispositional or moral orientations is inherently subjective with ideological undertones. Such evaluation of dispositions defined by moral stances is perceived by some as representing liberal bias or intimidating teacher candidates to comply with a preconceived set of moral beliefs determined by academia. The National Association of Scholars is a non-profit, politically conservative advocacy group, with interest in specific educational issues. These include academic content, unfairness, academic integrity, campus culture, and attitudes. The association went so far as to file a complaint with the Education Department stating that morally based and biased language within accreditation leads to standards that violate students' First Amendment rights (Powers, 2006). Stories can be found in the public press related to this moral focus on social justice and its potential indoctrination of students. The stories include one about a candidate who wrote a paper for his classroom-management course advocating the use of corporal punishment. His college of education dismissed him from the program citing the differences between his beliefs and the program goals as the cause. Later, the state Court of Appeals ruled that this violated the student's due process rights, and he was reinstated (Wilkerson, 2006). Another anecdote describes a student who failed four "professional disposition evaluations." The intervention to address this failure was requiring the candidate to sign a contract with the college of education. The contract targeted required activities in areas in need of dispositional improvement including mandatory diversity training. A complaint was filed with the Foundation for Individual Rights in Education, a conservative organization that seeks to defend and sustain individual rights at America's colleges and universities, including freedom of speech, religious liberty, and sanctity of conscience. The student was then told by college officials that he did not have to sign the contract and would not be expelled (Leo, 2005). William Damon, in a Fordham Foundation commentary, argued that dispositional frameworks could lead to narrow ideological impositions. The National Council for Accreditation of Teacher Education, now CAEP, maintains that standards focusing on candidates' dispositions are a reasonable, defensible, and valuable component of quality teacher education programs (Borko, Liston, & Whitcomb, 2007). However, others suggest that incorporating dispositions in a curriculum or assessment system, causes teacher education programs to run the risk of being viewed as supporting a social or political agenda of indoctrination (Hess, 2006) and that "Ultimately, screening on 'dispositions' serves primarily to cloak academia's biases in the garb of professional necessity" (Borko et al., 2007, p. 362). The controversy around social justice as a disposition highlights a fundamental challenge concerning the definition of teacher dispositions: Do dispositions relate more to observable behaviors or the less tangible aspects of teaching, like teachers' attitudes, beliefs, values and morals (Stooksberry, Schussler, & Bercaw, 2009)?

Teacher preparation programs are reluctant to grapple with the tough issues and challenges inherent to embracing moral education. This results in limitation of the discussion and teaching of desirable moral traits and dispositions, although they are inherent to becoming and acting as a good teacher. As Fenstermacher and Richardson (2005) indicated, quality teaching is both morally good and successful. Quality teaching is about how content is taught. Not only must the content be appropriate, proper, and aimed at some worthy purpose, but also the methods employed have to be morally defensible and grounded in shared conceptions of reasonableness. Further, the majority of candidate problems that arise within field experiences are not related to pedagogy or content knowledge, but rather to dispositions. As Osguthorpe (2013) stated:

> The core issue is almost always dispositional in nature and related to the moral and ethical manner in which the student teacher carries out the practice of teaching. In other words, the mentor teacher's worries might initially be voiced as a concern about instructional method, but they often are more closely connected to a concern about a student teacher's way of being and moral disposition—the student teacher's

level of responsibility, commitment, open-mindedness, care, kindness, politeness, or some other conception of dispositions. (p. 25)

Osguthorpe continues to state that teacher candidates are typically "counseled out" of teacher preparation, or later fired as teachers, due to a lack of self-awareness, integrity, persistence, care, commitment, relatedness, or civility. In spite of this, intentionality in developing these attributes is largely missing from teacher preparation and professional development opportunities. It is easier to skirt the issue than to address it. Ultimately, morality is wed to developing dispositional capacities to be responsive to students in multiple ways in a variety of contexts. The purpose of exploring teachers' personal beliefs and self-identity is to better understand how teacher candidates receive and process information and experiences. This helps us to understand how teachers are inclined to think and act when confronted with different teaching situations, and develop awareness of how their dispositions influence their thinking and actions related to teaching (Stooksberry et al., 2009). The moral dimensions of teaching can be examined within relationships and how a teacher responds to students (Sherman, 2006). This focus may be a beginning place to address the different concerns about moral aspects of educator dispositions, without completely avoiding their examination because of related controversy.

It is difficult to quantify or even "measure" the less technical aspects of teachers and teaching. Educator dispositions call for the opposite of analyzing a teacher's technical skills and knowledge. Instead, a focus on dispositions implies an examination of the minds of teachers, their ways of knowing, and their beliefs and attitudes that affect their decision-making, relationships and actions in the classroom. The complexities of examining a teacher's ways of thinking, as well as its ambiguous nature, has led to a continued lack of an agreed-upon definition of teacher dispositions. However, that does not negate their importance, especially if we are to define teaching as more than a technical implementation of a sequenced, mandated curriculum. Teaching dispositions can be an essential part of the value added by teacher preparation. Dispositions may cause the difference between the professional educator we need in the classroom and the layperson who comes in, perhaps with good intentions, but without necessary preparation. The intentional definition and cultivation of professional dispositions essential to an exemplary, highly qualified teacher, remains a largely unilluminated benefit of professional preparation. One of the challenges is that dispositions remain ill defined. Multiple definitions and perspectives associated with teacher dispositions including tendencies, values, habits of mind, attitudes, morals and behaviors have made it difficult to establish the usefulness of dispositions as a concept and to build a common research base (Ritchhart, 2001).

Even though dispositions are not well defined, they are important. In order for teachers to be more than mere 'cogs' in the educational machine, they must possess the dispositions necessary to teach and reach students (Wenzlaff, 1998). The lack of a clear understanding of and ongoing dialogue about dispositions often leads to a definition settling for "professional" behaviors on checklists such as promptness and appropriate dress. In some cases, dispositional measures have become verbatim statements of CAEP/NCATE language, devoid of shared meaning and application within the teacher preparation program (Thornton, 2006). It may be difficult to move beyond the technical aspect of teaching and to delve further into what dispositions mean and to talk about the greater implications of teaching and evaluating dispositions.

Defining dispositions beyond the technical skills of teaching is not a novel idea. Katz's (1993) work on dispositions focuses on patterns of behaviors that are exhibited frequently and intentionally in the absence of coercion. This builds on Dewey's (1933) work, which addresses the need to cultivate of the habits of mind necessary to effective teaching. Studies related to the characteristics of effective teachers (Demmon-Berger, 1986) and those of exemplary teachers (Collinson, 1996) have attempted to identify what teachers bring to the enterprise of teaching beyond knowledge and skills, that positively impacts students and learning. Katz and Raths (1985) distinguish dispositions from habits, stating that a habit refers to acts that are neither intentional nor consequent to reflection and suggesting that the term disposition be used to refer to a pattern of acts that are intentional on the part of the teacher, in a particular context and at particular times (Freeman, 2007). Distinguishing between dispositions and abilities may also help us to build a better understanding of dispositions. Dispositions and abilities are certainly related. In fact, some abilities may be deemed essential for the development of certain dispositions. For example, to develop the disposition to think critically, a student may need to cultivate the abilities to make inferences and evaluate arguments grounded in evidence. We may think of abilities as capacities to perform tasks, whereas dispositions describe how those abilities are manifested (Carducci, 2006).

Beyond considering habits of mind and professional characteristics, the concept of dispositions as one's perception of events has been widely embraced. Chandler's (1998) dispositional work focuses on the notion of self-examination of one's mind-set and the ability to reframe this. Many regard Combs' (1969) Florida studies of self-perceptions of effective helping professionals as seminal work that informs current efforts to define and evaluate dispositions. Combs utilizes an approach in which candidates respond in writing to a written human relations incident and classroom observations. This shows teacher candidates' perceptions of themselves in relation to others and the greater world, thus providing insight into their dispositions. Such reflective and perceptual processes are often used for program pre-admission screening and program embedded assessment of dispositions. Reflective journaling about one's beliefs as an educator may be used to evidence changes in a candidate's dispositions throughout a program. Unfortunately, perceptual-based approaches to dispositions are limited by their reliance on candidates' self-reporting and their ability to express meta-cognitive understanding. Studying evidence of how dispositions are actually manifested in the candidate's actions while teaching may build a bridge between the candidate's insights, or habits of mind, and student learning.

2   *Dispositions in Action*

Dispositions animate, motivate, and direct abilities and are present in the patterns of one's frequently exhibited behavior (Ritchhart, 2001). These behaviors may be thought of as *Dispositions in Action* (Thornton, 2006). This construct is not focused on personality traits, minimal behavior expectations, or self-reported values, but rather patterns of thought about issues of morals, ethics, and values which are revealed through interactions between teachers and students...how one is disposed to think and act as an educator. It is concerned with how dispositions influence decisions teachers make in the classroom and how they affect students as learners. It examines what teachers choose to do, not just what they are able to do. Norris (2003) helps distinguish abilities from dispositions further. An ability is a competency to perform a certain type of task physical or mental at a certain level of proficiency. Dispositions are the tendency to use these abilities. For example, some individuals have the ability to accurately assess the reliability of evidence within a study, and use that ability when designing or reviewing a study. While there may be other individuals who have this ability to tend not to use it (Freeman, 2003).

In order to learn about various dispositions, we need to have a framework that we can use to help us understand what we mean by the term. The *Dispositions in Action* framework allows us to examine dispositions within the nature of teaching and learning. *Dispositions in Action* (Thornton, 2006) may be thought of as a link between perception and practice. The construct evolved from grounded theory (Lincoln & Guba, 1985) involving studies of exemplary teachers using observation and discourse analysis (Faircloth, 1989) in real classrooms. Evidence of teacher dispositions can be found within classroom dialogue and teacher interactions with students. Discourse analysis provides a means to examine the conversations of ordinary lives, settings, and occasions to find how meaning, and structure are assembled and achieved (Macbeth, 2003). Sustained observation is important when assessing *Dispositions in Action*, as dispositions can be evidenced for longer and shorter periods of time, and do not go in and out of being very rapidly (Freeman, 2007). DIA can be a means to make explicit the implicit dispositions and related beliefs that educators hold based on evidence found in classroom interactions.

3   Why *Dispositions in Action* May Be Useful

Dispositions in Action offer a starting point to think about and use the definition of dispositions differently. *Dispositions in Action* can be thought of as habits of mind, including both cognitive and affective attributes, which are manifested within relationships as meaning-making occurs with others. They are evidenced through interactions in the form of discourse and nonverbal communicative interaction. Dispositions act as a filter of one's knowledge, skills, and beliefs, thus influencing the decisions and actions one takes in the classroom or professional setting. They may be helpful in determining both present and future teacher behaviors as (Mumford, 1998) dispositions act as explanations of past events and grounds for the prediction of future ones. Much like the work of Combs (1969), *Dispositions in Action* are developed from grounded theory and help to describe what teachers actually do in practice. Combs' work is derived from studies of helping professions, later translated to teaching. The concept of *Dispositions in Action* emerged from the work of classroom teachers. Validation studies were completed with groups of exemplary teachers, pre-service teachers and researchers in the field. Public school students also participated in the development of the definitions and descriptions of the dispositions. Students' perceptions of effective teachers and how teacher's language affected student learning were central to the initial study that led to developing *Dispositions in Action*. These multiple perspectives and lenses helped to establish face validity (Lincoln & Guba, 1985) and supported the iterative development of the concept via analysis of language and interactions. Connections between *Dispositions in Action* and resulting student learning were examined using The Structure of the Observed Learning Outcomes, or SOLO, taxonomy (Biggs & Collis, 1989) to evaluate depth and complexity of student thinking.

4   Connections to Other Teacher Quality Frameworks

The DIA concept can be readily connected to several areas of educational thought about teacher characteristics and quality. These include Schön's (1987) reflective practice, developmentally responsive practices (NMSA), Palmer's (1987) writings about the teacher as self and the works of Dewey and others.

Unlike many other teacher disposition models, *Dispositions in Action* are about how dispositions determine what happens in classroom practice and thus, student learning outcomes. It helps us to explore the question, "What do dispositions have to do with teaching, and ultimately, student learning?" *Dispositions in Action* parallel other models of evaluating effective teaching practices. A comparison of *Dispositions in Action* to the Dialogue of Adaptive Expertise (Bransford, Brown, & Cocking, 2000) helps to bring the dialogic and relationship base of responsive DIA to light. Parallels in practice and use of language are indicated in Table 3.1 below.

TABLE 3.1   *Adaptive expertise and responsive dispositions.*

Dialogue of adaptive expertise		Dialogue of a responsive disposition	
Assessment centered	– Formative assessments to make student thinking visible – Provides necessary feedback	*Assessment*	– Critiques student work Sets goals – Challenges students to move beyond & articulate why
Learner centered	– Diagnostic teaching – Cultural responsiveness – Individual differences	*Management*	– Empowers students to make decisions, think & own the classroom environment – Connects students to build a sense of community, ownership, belongingness & value of diversity
Knowledge centered	– Encourages students to make sense of information – Builds on prior knowledge – Promotes authentic problem solving	*Curriculum & instruction*	– Facilitates the understanding of individuals based on learner needs – Supports students understanding via scaffolding & connection – Creative in differentiation of instruction/variety/ connecting to students & the real world

TABLE 3.1   *Adaptive expertise and responsive dispositions (cont.).*

Dialogue of adaptive expertise		Dialogue of a responsive disposition	
Community centered	– Includes the classroom as a community, the school as a community, and the degree to which students, teachers, and administrators feel connected to the "larger community"	*Professional roles*	– Works to advocate for change in the professional community – Inclusive of all members of the learning community and builds on shared ownership, participation & voice

Connections can also be made to Combs's (1969) original studies on dispositions and ensuing study of educators' perceptions (Wasicsko, 2007) which examine one's thinking and perceptual understandings. Based on these studies, The National Network for the Study of Educator Dispositions utilizes the "Teacher effectiveness research: A perceptual approach" manual and assessment tools as a major strand of their research in the field of teacher dispositions. Parallels between effective members of the helping professions and responsively disposed teachers are illustrated in Table 3.2.

TABLE 3.2   *Florida studies in the helping professions and Dispositions in Action.*

Teacher effective research: a perceptual approach (Florida studies)	*Dispositions in Action*
Perception of self as identified (self)	Management enacted as self connected to students
Perception of others as able (others)	Assessment enacted as high expectations
People oriented (purpose)	Curriculum & instruction enacted as responsive
Perception of purpose as larger (frame of reference)	Professional roles enacted as change driven

Responsive *Dispositions in Action* can also be correlated to Danielson's (2013) Framework for Effective Practice.

TABLE 3.3   *Danielson and Dispositions in Action.*

Danielson framework	*Dispositions in Action* (responsive)
Domain 3: Instruction Substantive feedback (3d)	Critical
Domain 2: Classroom Environment Expectations for learning (2b)	Challenging
Domain 3: Instruction Flexibility (3e)	Facilitative
Domain 3: Instruction Responsiveness (3e)	Creative
Domain 2: Classroom Environment Respect (2a)	Empowering
Domain 2: Classroom Environment Rapport (2a)	Connected
Domain 4: Professional Responsibilities Relationships with colleagues (4d)	Collaborative
Domain 4: Professional Responsibilities Advocacy (4f)	Change-Driven

Dispositions are a critical aspect of a well-prepared, highly qualified teacher and correlate with teaching practices. Defining what we, as a profession, mean by dispositions and delineating and describing how they affect and are demonstrated in practice may be increasingly important in a context where the value of professionally prepared teachers is often negated by policy and accountability practices. Determining how these dispositions are exhibited by exemplary teachers, and working to articulate and evidence how teacher preparation intentionally cultivates and evidences dispositions as related to best practices is an important part of demonstrating the value added of teacher preparation. Using a definition that is demonstrated within, but distinct from teaching practices, can allow and examination of how a teacher's dispositions affect student learning, This can move the thinking about dispositions away from simply linking them to standards language for the purposes of accountability and data production, or reducing them to a list of normative behaviors. An orientation of technical rationality limits the depth and promise of research and evaluation of dispositions as praxis. Moving the construct of dispositions beyond teachers' self-perceptions and reflections can reveal how these habits of mind, or dispositions toward thinking, actually affect teaching and learning. *Dispositions in Action* allows the conversation and articulation of the role of dispositions in teacher preparation to move into an epistemology of practice, much like that of reflection in action (Schön, 1987).

5   Can Dispositions Be Taught?

If we are able to establish the importance of teacher dispositions and develop a way to observe and assess them, the next logical step is to figure out how to teach these dispositions to future educators and to veteran teachers through professional development experiences. I consider teacher dispositions to be one of the most important, if not the most important, thing that I teach to preservice and masters level students in my classes. This begs the question, "Can dispositions be taught or are they inherent within an individual and thus intractable?" Content knowledge and pedagogical skills make up the majority of a preparation program. These elements can be readily recognized and developed through instructional design, and a student's growth in these areas can be documented to evidence success. We have no doubt that we teach future educators about the content that they need to understand and about the practices that will make up their repertoire of teaching. When it comes to dispositions, we *think* we are teaching them to our students. We can sense it. We can feel it. We model it and deconstruct it. Dispositions are interwoven within a myriad of experiences in teacher preparation classrooms. It is somewhat like a hidden curriculum. It is there. It is being taught. However, it is not clearly or effectively evidenced and assessed.

How do we teach dispositions as compared to content and pedagogy? Like abilities and motivation, dispositions are subject to alteration through example, direct teaching, explicit scaffolding, and practice. Dispositions require justification and students need to be given reasons why consistent behaviors and thoughts of certain types are important to their teaching. Overtime, building knowledge, understanding, and honing skills to interact effectively can cause candidates to leave programs with changes in their dispositions (Diez, 2006). Often assessment of educator dispositions is considered diagnostic. Dispositional analysis brings things to light that might cause the candidate to make a choice such as moving to another career or solidify the candidate's choice to engage in further learning necessary to develop the knowledge and skills required to change the disposition (Diez, 2002). The development of specific skills and abilities may be deemed essential for the development of certain dispositions. For example, to develop the disposition to think critically, an individual may need to cultivate the abilities to make inferences and evaluate arguments grounded in evidence (Carducci, 2006). The manifestation of dispositions can be influenced. Intentional consideration of the conditions under which dispositions are taught is important to any learning related to dispositional development. Dispositions can be triggered or obstructed by conditions external to the person. Teacher preparation could therefore could focus on triggering and enhancing dispositions (Riveros, Norris, Hayward, & Phillips, 2012) to affect how they are manifested in the classroom. Developments and changes in dispositions are grounded in understanding of the self. Developing skills and abilities related to self-examination is necessary to developing dispositions. Parker Palmer (1997) focuses on the development of personal identity and integrity. She sees the development of teacher dispositions as following a series of discernment about the self in relationship to the role of a teacher. Oja and Reiman (2007) suggest the usefulness of teacher educators adopting a developmental perspective when thinking about the nurturing and assessment of educator dispositions. They use a three faceted view of teacher development including conceptual development, ego development, and moral development and teach to student's developmental levels and needs. The skills of self-examination and reflection can influence our interactions and relationships with others. A focus on developing the skill sets and abilities to create effective relationships with others is important to teaching dispositions. Given the developmental nature of candidate dispositions and the complex nature of teaching, the assessment of dispositions may require being guided by what Diez (2006) calls an epistemology of mind. He defines this as a culture of assessment using qualitative, interpretivist approaches to look at individual teacher candidates' responses to the challenges of becoming a teacher.

Dispositions can be intentionally taught and become a cornerstone of educator preparation with approaches that develop foundational skills, engage candidates in analyzing their personal identity and the role of the teacher, and understanding the why behind responses to different conditions and situations across teaching and moral domains. Qualitatively assessing dispositions with the *Dispositions in Action* model can better enable us to begin to develop a cumulative picture of the candidates' readiness for teaching at the point at which a summative decision must be made (Hare, 2007). The research and literature on educator dispositions is often centered on identifying dispositions and using them to make decisions about applying to or continuing in teacher preparation programs. Thus, this becomes the impetus for colleges of education attempting to clearly articulate and evaluate their own lists of identified dispositions. We can move beyond this. If we are to assess them, we need to move towards an examination of how dispositions are taught within our programs. The question of whether dispositions are innate and intractable, or malleable and able to be instilled and cultivated is still being investigated, but the emerging literature suggests dispositions can indeed be changed. If this is the case, we may need to ask our teacher preparation and professional development programs to help to assure that teachers develop desired dispositions, rather than merely espouse and document them.

6   Do Context and Content Matter?

If we are intentionally able to teach students desired dispositions, how does
this affect their teaching practices once they graduate? I began to wonder what
would happen next, when candidates enter the field as beginning teachers.
I investigated this within one of my studies to find out. I was often told that
teachers' content areas have a profound influence on their dispositions.
Language Arts and Social Studies teachers are said to have more opportunities
to develop relationships and in-depth understanding with their students,
while Math and Science teachers had to focus more carefully on the facts
and procedures. I also gathered, from multiple conversations and anecdotal
data, that educators thought that you could only be responsive and connected
to students if you taught in the right kind of school and in the right kind of
place. A teacher could think and behave a certain way with students who were
gifted, affluent or primarily located in white suburban schools with "good"
parents. These students were ready for student-centered, engaged learning. In
contrast, teachers in more culturally diverse or poorer urban and rural settings
often told me that "those kind of kids" would take advantage of anything
different that you tried to do. There needed to be control and quiet so students
wouldn't get out of hand. Didactic learning wasn't necessarily seen as the
teacher's choice, but rather, the school context demanded it.

I decided to look more closely into the impact context and climate had
on how teachers were disposed to think about and implement teaching and
define learning. I chose to follow new teachers who had just graduated from a
middle level teacher preparation program that intentionally sought to develop
responsive dispositions. I was able to observe and interview a cadre of six teachers
in their junior year, student teaching experience, first, and fourth year teaching
to evaluate their *Dispositions in Action* over time. These teachers taught across
various content disciplines and within urban, rural and suburban districts to
allow for comparison of how these new teachers evidenced their dispositions
within their classroom environments. They all faced the challenge to teach well
and use best practices, in spite of the pressures of standardized testing. When all
was said and done, content area and school context were not significant factors
when correlated with teacher DIA. Those who exited their preparation program
with responsive dispositions maintained those dispositions in schools where
it was the norm to be progressive and in schools that were more traditional
and teacher centered. Teachers working in suburban schools maintained their
dispositions, as did the new teachers who taught in schools with more varied or
lower socioeconomic status and diverse ethnicities. The responsively disposed
teachers were able to evidence their responsive *Dispositions in Action* within
their classrooms, regardless of content area. Contrary to popular opinion,

even the Math teachers. If you are responsibly disposed, that is how you are going to teach in any context. In addition, one's dispositions are sustained over time, this may increase their impact in the teaching field. The most significant change in the teachers' dispositions occurred during their professional teacher preparation classes. This then carried over into their teaching practices in the field up through their fourth year of classroom practice.

7   What about Collaboration and Shared Vision?

Years later, I found myself looking at teacher quality within charter schools. The emphasis on and number of charter schools throughout the nation was rapidly increasing. Some charter schools had been successful in evidencing student growth and learning while others were not. I worked with key informants to observe and locate four effective charter schools within our region where I conducted case studies, observations and interviews. The commonalities shared among the schools, beyond being public charter schools, was that they worked with middle grade students, demonstrated academic success, and had indicators of positive climate such as high attendance rates, low discipline referrals, and substantial parental interaction and involvement. The identified schools used responsive practices grounded in philosophies that aligned with developmentally responsive teaching, and potentially related responsive dispositions. Schools chosen for the case study represented suburban, urban, and rural contexts. The sizes of the school varied from the inner city school with over 1,000 students with 71 % reported as an ethnic minority and 54% of all students receiving free lunch, to the small rural school with 186 students, with 97.3% Caucasian students and 19.4% of students receiving free lunch. I wanted to know what made some charter schools effective in terms of meaningful student learning while others were not. Themes emerged across the study schools giving insight into their shared and differing characteristics. One common theme across these effective charter schools was that of shared vision and collaboration among faculty, administration, students, parents and community. However, even within the schools where teachers were hired based on a shared vision, some teachers demonstrated that vision through their classroom practices and interactions differently than others. Again, dispositions were coming into play.

Dispositions can be more clearly articulated and defined using models and constructs that are grounded in emergent theory and generated in real classrooms with real teachers and real students. How teacher dispositions affect the nature of learning needs to be the focus. Educator dispositions are especially important in this age where teaching is being reduced to technical actions and behaviors and student success is defined by standardized tests. If teachers are to be more than cogs in a machine, identification and cultivation of responsive dispositions is necessary.

So what have we learned? The use of the *Dispositions in Action* model allows us to identify connections between and among teacher quality frameworks as we examine the habits of mind that undergird the decisions teachers make. Dispositions can be altered by teaching the skills and abilities that lead to thoughtful understanding of the self and of the conditions that affect dispositional orientation and teacher choices. Responsive dispositions can occur within and across schools representing various contexts and challenges. Responsive teacher dispositions result in student learning that promotes mindfulness through critical thinking and student voice and reasoned decision-making. These teachers focus on deep understanding of content and its application to the real world. They emphasize respecting differences and learning how to negotiate with others in the best interest of all members of a learning community. Better understanding and cultivation of responsive dispositions may be critical to developing teacher role models who inspire youth to become adults who can positively affect our society and world.

Think again:

1 How would you explain the concept of teacher dispositions in general to someone else? How would you explain the concept of *Dispositions in Action?*
2 Do you believe that dispositions can be taught? Should they be?
3 What have you learned about dispositions that make sense and resonates with you? What do you still question about dispositions?

References

Biggs, J., & Collis, K. (1989). Towards a model of school-based curriculum development and assessment using the SOLO taxonomy. *Australian Journal of Education, 33*(2), 151–163.

Borko, H., Liston, D., & Whitcomb, J. A. (2007). Apples and fishes: The debate over dispositions in teacher education. *Journal of Teacher Education, 58*(5), 359–364.

Bransford, J. D., Brown, A. L., & Cocking, R. R. (2000). *How people learn: Brain, mind experience, and school.* Washington, DC: The National Academies Press.

CAEP. (2017). *Standard 3: Candidate quality, recruitment, and selectivity: Rationale. Commission on standards and performance reporting.* Retrieved from http://caepnet.org/standards/standard-3/rationale

Campbell, E. (2003). *The ethical teacher.* Buckingham: Open University Press.

Carducci, B. J. (2006). *The psychology of personality.* Oxford: Blackwell.

Chandler, T. A. (1998). Use of reframing as a classroom strategy. *Education, 119*(2), 365–366.

Collinson, V. (1996, July). *Becoming an exemplary teacher: Integrating professional, interpersonal, and intrapersonal knowledge.* Paper presented at the Annual Meeting of the Japan-United States Teacher Education Consortium, Naruto.

Combs, A. W. (1969). *Florida studies in the helping professions.* Gainesville, FL: University of Florida Press.

Demmon-Berger, D. (1986). *Effective teaching: Observations from research.* Arlington, VA: American Association of School Administrators.

Dewey, J. (1933). *How we think: A restatement of the relation of reflective thinking to the educative process.* Boston, MA: D.C. Heath and company.

Diez, M. E. (2002). The certification connection: Licensure ought to guarantee that every classroom comes equipped with a skilled knowledgeable teacher. The new performance standards for teachers are making that possible. (Forum). *Education Next, 1*(8).

Diez, M. E. (2006). Assessing dispositions: Context and questions. *New Educator, 2*(1), 57–72.

Faircloth, N. (1989). *Language and power.* London: Longman.

Fenstermacher, G. D., & Richardson, V. (2005). On making determinations of quality in teaching. *Teachers College Record, 107*(1), 186–213.

Framework for Teaching. (2013). *Danielson group.* Retrieved September 1, 2017, from http://www.danielsongroup.org/framework/

Freeman, L. (2003, November). *Where did dispositions come from and what can we do with them.* Paper presented at the Second Annual Symposium on Educator Dispositions, Eastern Kentucky University, Richmond, KY.

Freeman, L. (2007). An overview of dispositions in teacher education. In M. E. Diez & J. Raths (Eds.), *Dispositions in teacher education* (pp. 3–29). Charlotte, NC: Information Age.

Hare, S. (2007). We teach who we are: The intersection of teacher formation and educator dispositions. In M. Diez & J. Raths (Eds.), *Dispositions in teacher education* (pp. 139–152). Charlotte, NC: IAP Inc.

Hess, F. M. (2006, February 5). Schools of reeducation. *Washington Post, 5,* B07.

Katz, L. G. (1993). Dispositions as educational goals. *ERIC Digest.* Retrieved May 1, 2016, from http://eric.ed.gov/?id=ED363454

Katz, L. G., & Raths, J. D. (1985). Dispositions as goals for teacher education. *Teaching and Teacher Education, 1*(4), 301–307.

Leo, J. (2005). Class (room) warriors. *US News and World Report, 139*(15), 75.

Lincoln, Y. S., & Guba, E. G. (1985). *Naturalistic inquiry* (Vol. 75). Newbury Park, CA: Sage Publications.

Macbeth, D. (2003). Hugh Mehan's learning lessons reconsidered: On the differences between the naturalistic and critical analysis of classroom discourse. *American Educational Research Journal, 40*(1), 239–280.

Mumford, S. (2003). *Dispositions*. Oxford: Oxford University Press.

Norris, J. A. (2003). Looking at classroom management through a social and emotional learning lens. *Theory Into Practice, 42*(4), 313–318.

Oja, S. N., & Reiman, A. J. (2007). A constructivist-developmental perspective. In M. E. Diez & J. Raths (Eds.), *Dispositions in teacher education* (pp. 93–117). Charlotte, NC: Information Age Publishing.

Osguthorpe, R. D. (2013). Attending to ethical and moral dispositions in teacher education. *Issues in Teacher Education, 22*(1), 17.

Palmer, P. J. (1987). Community, conflict, and ways of knowing: Ways to deepen our educational agenda. *Change: The Magazine of Higher Learning, 19*(5), 20–25.

Palmer, P. J. (1997). The heart of a teacher identity and integrity in teaching. *Change: The Magazine of Higher Learning, 29*(6), 14–21.

Powers, E. (2006, June 6). A spirited disposition debate. *Inside Higher Ed.* Retrieved August 22, 2017, from https://www.insidehighered.com/news/2006/06/06/disposition

Ritchhart, R. (2001). From IQ to IC: A dispositional view of intelligence. *Roeper Review, 23*(3), 143–150.

Riveros, A., Norris, S., Hayward, D., & Phillips, L. (2012). Dispositions and the quality of learning. In J. Kirby & M. Lawson (Eds.), *Enhancing the quality of learning: Dispositions, instruction, and learning processes.* Cambridge: Cambridge University Press. doi:10.1017/CBO9781139048224.005

Sanger, M. N., & Osguthorpe, R. D. (2011). Teacher education, preservice teacher beliefs, and the moral work of teaching. *Teaching and Teacher Education, 27*(3), 569–578.

Sherman, S. (2006). Moral dispositions in teacher education: Making them matter. *Teacher Education Quarterly, 33*(4), 41–57.

Schön, D. A. (1987). *Educating the reflective practitioner: Toward a new design for teaching and learning in the professions.* San Francisco, CA: Jossey-Bass.

Stooksberry, L. M., Schussler, D. L., & Bercaw, L. A. (2009). Conceptualizing dispositions: Intellectual, cultural, and moral domains of teaching. *Teachers and Teaching: Theory and Practice, 15*(6), 719–736.

Thornton, H. (2006). Dispositions in action: Do dispositions make a difference in practice? *Teacher Education Quarterly, 33*(2), 53–68.

Wasicsko, M. M. (2007). *The national network for the study of educator dispositions.* Retrieved February 3, 2017, from http://www.educatordispositions.org/moodle/moodle/mod/resource/view.php?id=4

Wenzlaff, T. L. (1998). Dispositions and portfolio development: Is there a connection? *Education, 118*(4), 564–573.

Wilkerson, J. R. (2006). Measuring teacher dispositions: Standards-based or morality-based. *Teachers College Record.* Retrieved April 20, 2006, from http://www.tcrecrod.org

How Do Dispositions Align with Child Development?

Think about:

1 What theories and approaches to understanding childhood development do you know about or embrace?
2 What do you consider the most challenging aspects of childhood development for elementary aged children? Adolescents?
3 What is the link between student development and teacher dispositions?

∙∙∙

A key to being successful in reaching and teaching students of all ages is matching teaching practices and approaches to the developmental nature of students in each classroom. As we have examined in previous chapters, using a certain type of teaching approach or specific practice deemed to fit student development may not be enough, as dispositions determine how these practices come to life in the classroom. Here we explore how accepted systems of thought about human learning and explicit cultivation of supporting teacher dispositions link. This linkage illuminates the need for explicit attention to dispositional development of teachers, as evidenced within various theoretical frames of human learning. Responsive dispositions support teaching and learning that is intentionally designed to address specific characteristics and meet specific student needs, as learners progress through developmental stages.

1 Child Development in the Elementary School Years

Teachers of young children are often held in high regard for their ability to truly care for the children they teach. From time a child is born, relationships and interactions with adults are critical to child development and learning. A teacher's moment-by-moment actions and interactions with children are the most powerful determinant of learning outcomes and development (Copple & Bredekamp, 2009).

© KONINKLIJKE BRILL NV, LEIDEN, 2018 | DOI 10.1163/9789004364486_004

Interactions with others, including peers, and the social and cultural contexts in which this interaction happens, is significant. The values, expectations, and behavioral and linguistic conventions that shape children's lives help to determine if learning experiences in school are meaningful (Copple & Bredekamp, 2009). The importance of teachers' dispositions in the early grades is not to be overlooked. Teachers that are well suited to teach young children in elementary school exhibit personality characteristics and behaviors that focus on nurturing, guiding, and supporting young learners as they progress from kindergarten through elementary school. Teacher preparation programs and professional development often focus on developmental characteristics of these young learners by studying child development experts such as Jean Piaget, Lev Vygotsky, and Maria Montessori.

Jean Piaget is best known for his stage theory of cognitive development. Piaget's (1964) work and its implication for teaching children is typically a foundational part of teacher preparation. It can be found within child psychology and development courses and ensuing courses focusing on instructional design and the learning environment. Piaget noted that one's reality is a dynamic system of continuous change namely, transformations and states. Understanding this change involves two basic functions: assimilation, which is the process of fitting new information into pre-existing cognitive schemas and accommodation, where new information in one's environment alters pre-existing cognitive schemas. In essence, as we acquire new understandings we mold them to fit our current worldviews and beliefs or alter our current worldviews and beliefs to adapt to the acceptance and accommodation of the new information. According to Piaget, these changes occur within four levels of cognitive development including the sensorimotor, preoperational, concrete operational and formal operational periods. Sensorimotor cognition involves the progressive construction of knowledge and understanding of the world by coordinating experiences (such as vision and hearing) with physical interactions with objects (such as grasping, sucking, and stepping). Infants gain knowledge of the world from the physical actions they perform within it. During the preoperational stage, children do not yet understand concrete logic and cannot mentally manipulate information as it increasingly becomes represented by symbols. In the next stage, the concrete operational, children's behavior is characterized by the appropriate use of logic, however hypothetical thinking is not yet developed and only problems that apply to concrete events or objects can be solved. When individuals enter the formal operational stage, their intelligence is demonstrated through the logical use of symbols related to abstract concepts and the use of hypothetical and deductive reasoning. During this time, people develop the ability to think critically about abstract concepts. Piaget's model of cognitive development is sequential, as individuals must experience one stage before moving onto the next.

Vygotsky is known for his Social Development Theory that states social interaction precedes development; consciousness and cognition are actually the end product of socialization and social behavior. Vygotsky's theory is foundational to constructivism, the concept that rather than acting as passive recipients of information people actually build their own understanding based on their prior experiences and lives. Vygotsky's work has three major themes: social interaction, the more knowledgeable other, and the zone of proximal development. Social interaction with a more knowledgeable other, who has a better conceptual understanding than the learner, such as a teacher or peer, plays a fundamental role in the process of cognitive development. This social learning precedes cognitive development. Learners also have a zone of proximal development, which is the optimal time for learning to occur. Vygotsky focused on the connections between people and the sociocultural context in which they interact. According to Vygotsky, humans use tools that develop from a culture, such as speech and writing, to mediate their social environments. At first, these social tools serve solely as ways to communicate needs to others, but the eventual internalization of these tools leads to the development of higher level thinking skills (Vygotsky, 1980).

Another expert in childhood development is Maria Montessori whose theory emphasizes individuality and independence in learning. Children are seen as inherently curious and learning driven. Education is viewed as a process that should occur organically and in harmony with the child's individual development. Montessori's theory includes five basic tenets. The first, *respect for the child*, allows children choices and prepares them to become independent learners as they discover the world through a hands-on approach. According to Montessori, children have an *absorbent mind* where learning is an inherent process in their everyday life. Children also become best able to learn different skills at specific points in their development which she calls *sensitive periods* that vary from individual to individual and provide the best time to introduce new concepts and skills. The physical organization of a Montessori classroom focuses on having a *prepared environment* that is filled with pleasing, available, and well-organized materials that the teacher wants the child to experience. The final tenant of her theory is that children should educate themselves to develop the skills necessary for life within this prepared environment. They should make choices and assist each other as they learn. Montessori labels this *autoeducation* (Montessori, 2013).

The disposition for a teacher to promote independent thinking, value socially constructed knowledge, and encourage the social interactions and language that underlie these theories is important to the learning of elementary-aged children. Piaget was a proponent of independent thinking and critical of the standardized teacher-centered instruction that is an increasingly common practice in schools (Crain, 2015). Child-centered classrooms in which the teacher makes instructional choices to respond to varied individual needs and the concept of "open education" are direct applications of Piaget's views (Wadsworth, 1996).

According to Open Education (2017):

> The open classroom, at its best, is a busy laboratory, richly provisioned with materials for learning. Alone or in small groups, children move from one work area to another, using balance beams, colored beads, blocks, and other hands-on material in the mathematics corner; working on art projects in paint, clay, or construction scraps; reading quietly or aloud to others from books or from their own illustrated reports. The room itself is arranged into several separate learning centers, a functional organization that invites choice of participation in a variety of activities. The school day is flexibly scheduled, allowing students to determine for themselves when an activity merits more time and when it is completed.... The teacher rarely calls the entire class together for group instruction. ...the teacher circulates among students, extending their learning by commenting and responding to their work, asking leading questions, and suggesting further directions for them to explore.

The importance of the role of the teacher and the dispositions they evidence is emphasized by Vygotsky who states that a child at first follows an adult's example and then gradually develops the ability to do certain tasks without help, thus becoming more independent (Vygotsky, 1980, p. 86). Social interaction is the means to develop this increasing understanding and independence as children benefit from initiating and regulating their own learning activities and from interacting with their peers (Copple & Bredekamp, 2009). Maria Montessori's approach can be characterized by an emphasis on independence, freedom within limits, and respect for a child's natural psychological, physical, and social development (American Montessori Society, 2017). Student choice, learning through discovery and freedom to move and learn through interaction with others are all elements of classrooms that are representative of these developmental theorists' take on education designed to meet the needs of young learners.

As children progress through developmental stages, emergent themes and challenges can be identified as fundamental to their growth as human beings. Elementary-aged students progress from egocentrism to learning how to consider others' experiences and begin to dabble with the concept of empathy. The social connections and interactions among elementary-aged students are vital to their language development and the conceptual understanding they define within their concrete world of thinking. The importance of context and community, beyond the school, is clear. Learning experiences should be responsive to students as individuals and members of a larger community. Early on, elementary school children are dependent upon and concerned with their relationship to their parents and other significant caregiving adults. As children progress developmentally, the importance of being around friends, learning from them, and working to gradually, become more self-sufficient and independent increases. Language development is key to understanding the world around them. Play becomes a significant form of learning for students both within and outside of the classroom.

Play enables children to develop self-regulation of their behaviors and choices while it promotes language, cognition, and social competence. Play is important to the development of physical abilities and competencies as well as cognitive ones. Through play, children learn to understand and make sense of their world. This interaction with others enables children to learn to express and control emotions and develop their symbolic and problem-solving abilities (Davidson, 1998). Research indicates a correlation between children's play and the development of capacities that are critical to later learning, social competence, and success in school. These include not only self-regulation, but also symbolic thinking, memory and language development (Copple & Bredekamp, 2009).

The need to teach in ways that are responsive to children's developmental needs is evident in the research on child development and within NAEYC's, National Association for the Education of Young Children, framework for developmentally appropriate practices (Bredekamp, 1987). Elementary teachers need to be disposed to both support and encourage the social interactions, self-choice, authentic inquiry and play necessary to student growth and success. The responsive dispositions to be facilitative, empowering, and challenging, are clearly aligned with what elementary-aged students need in their teachers.

2   Adolescent Development

In contrast, to the positive reaction to those who have chosen to educate young children, when you state, "I teach middle school" it is likely you get a response of "God bless you!" or "Are you crazy?" It is not surprising to anyone who has worked with young adolescent learners that it takes a special kind of teacher to reach and teach young adolescents (and actually enjoy doing it). It requires a certain set of dispositions to be well matched with the needs and characteristics of both young adolescents and older adolescents throughout their middle and high school years. Responsively disposed teachers may be key to student success in the middle and high school classroom. The research is abundant and clear regarding the importance of developmentally responsive practices in middle school. Underlying the decision to teach responsively is a significant influence on how teaching practices come to life in the classroom, the teacher's dispositions.

Adolescence is a time of great change second only to the rate of change experienced by infants. Not only do young adolescents undergo significant physical change, but they are also changing socially, emotionally, and cognitively. Young adolescents undergo more rapid change and profound personal changes between 10 and 15 than any other time in their lives (NMSA, 2010). Due to this change, adolescence was once thought of as a time of "storm and stress" (Hall, 1904). Young adolescents were viewed as hormones on wheels, difficult, changing and moody. However, the transition from childhood to adulthood is relatively smooth (Arnett, 1999) and the changes adolescents undergo actually present an opportunity to positively impact the adults they become.

Up until the mid-20th century, adolescence was not a common concept. Children of this age often assumed adult roles of providing for their family and getting married. The transition to adulthood happened relatively rapidly in terms of social norms and expectations. A changing world and economy changed social expectations for adolescents. The need for a better-educated workforce, and the child welfare movement led to more children attending high school, delaying their entry into adult roles. In current times, there is an increasing expectation of students to pursue post-secondary degrees at community colleges or universities meanwhile the opportunity to easily find gainful employment is more limited. Now, adolescents spend more time with same-age peers and enter adulthood later than ever before. This changes the notion of what it means to be an adolescent (Nichols & Good, 2004). This extended concept of adolescence prolongs many of the challenges and transitions young people face. According to the ASCD Education Update (Checkley, 2004):

> They strive for independence, yet they clamor to belong. They fight the connections they have with their parents, but they need to form alliances with peers and bond with understanding teachers. They are finding themselves and, in the process, will challenge authority, experiment with sarcasm, and try on many different personalities. They are adolescents. And, if recent brain studies are accurate, they can be as young as age 10 or as old as age 25.

Indeed, there are inherent challenges for adolescents dealing with so much change at one time. Cognitively, they are moving between concrete and abstract thinking. They are developing their ability to reason and to question as they unearth complexities that used to seem simple. The adults they look to for knowing all of the answers suddenly seem not to have them anymore. They want and need the approval of these adults in their lives but at the same time wish to break away and become themselves. Socially they are trying to fit in but also be independent. They are trying to determine: Who am I in this world?

The development of identity and the search for belonging are driving forces in adolescence. Emotional changes are impacted by fluctuating hormonal balances and other physiological factors such as puberty and accelerated growth spurts. Social relationships complicate the management of emotions that these young people are still learning to control and master. They are beginning to navigate the complexity of moral decisions as they move from focusing on themselves to empathizing with others. They are "becoming" and then moving into young adulthood. At the same time, they are encountering a plethora of new cultural and societal opportunities, expectations and challenges. At no other time in life do so many shifts in development and social contexts occur simultaneously (Nichols, 2009). The complex and multifaceted task of helping adolescents navigate through the challenges of developing and understanding relationships with others while defining who they are, now and in the future, is further complicated by the social culture of today's society and the ever increasingly connected world.

It is a time of rapid change in our world. Eighty percent of all jobs our students will one day hold have not yet been invented. The overall amount of knowledge that exists is doubling every ten to twelve months, while it used to double every decade, then every few years. The adolescents in our classrooms might commonly live to be 120. So how do we prepare them for a world that does not yet exist? Adolescents do not need teachers who see themselves solely as dispensers of all there is to know about particular subjects. They need dynamic adults offering a solid core of current knowledge who also create the ability and inclination to learn more in the years ahead (Wormeli, 2009).

The main goal of education is therefore not memorizing or even understanding all of the content knowledge of the world in which we live. Rather, it is for adolescents to become fully functioning, actualized individuals. They need to become actively aware of the larger world and ask significant questions about it, while wrestling with big ideas. They need to be able to think rationally and critically, express their thoughts clearly to others, and to be deeply independent. They need to use digital tools to communicate and collaborate with the world and to learn from a variety of resources as they interpret information and embrace lifelong learning. They need to be good stewards of the Earth. They need to understand and use major concepts and skills across all content fields including physical education, music and the other arts to develop their own strengths and talents. Perhaps above all, they need to learn how to recognize and make responsible, ethical decisions and learn to value the diverse people and complex interdependent world in which they live. The development of both personal and social skills help adolescents assume responsibility for their actions and to become concerned about the impact of their choices on the welfare of others within our local, national, and global communities (NMSA, 2010).

3   Moral Development

The work of Lawrence Kohlberg may give us insight to another foundational developmental challenge that our students must work through. Moral development. It is thought to be crucial and essential to educating children. It is also controversial as it evokes questions of whose definition of morality is used, and who should be teaching it. Does the responsibility for moral development lie within the family and affiliated communities or do we expect students to learn to exhibit proper moral behaviors in school? This challenge may be particularly significant in today's world where apparently dichotomous paradigms exist, each defining what is moral and why, in their own terms to support their own beliefs and agendas. Moral tensions and dilemmas may perhaps be more evident now than they had even been in the past and we need a framework by which to understand them.

Kohlberg's (1981) theory of moral development stemmed from Piaget's work including his theory of moral reasoning. Individuals progress through stages of moral development that are built upon our cognitive stages of development. According to Kohlberg, morality can be developed either negatively or positively, depending on how an individual accomplishes the tasks before him during each stage of moral development across his lifespan. He used various scenarios to explore children's moral decision-making. His studies did not focus on asking whether or not the person in the situation was morally right or wrong, but rather sought out the reasons why the children thought that the individual in the scenario was morally right or not.

Kohlberg's theory encompasses three levels of moral development: preconventional, conventional, and postconventional. Each level has two distinct stages. Within the *preconventional level,* the sense of morality is externally controlled and grounded in rules, authority figures, and the consequences an action evokes. At this level, decisions are based on compliance to rules, and hoping to keep out of trouble. Stage (1) one of the preconventional level exhibits an obedience/punishment orientation to morality. People take specific actions to follow the rules and avoid punishments. The second (2) stage in this level is referred to as the instrumental relativist orientation. In this stage, the morality of a decision is judged by how the action satisfies the individual needs of the doer. For example, a child may state that it is morally right for someone to steal food if her children are hungry, or to take someone else's pencil because they want it. As an individual moves into the *conventional level* of moral decision-making, morality is largely define by personal and societal relationships. The rules of authority figures are still accepted but not in fear of punishment but rather because individuals believe the rules are necessary to maintain positive relationships and societal order. There are two stages within the conventional level (3 and 4). The first stage (3) in this level can be labeled the good boy/girl orientation. Here moral judgments are grounded in interpersonal relationships based on societal roles and expectations. Decisions are largely placed on what a "nice" person would do, for example, sharing your lunch with a friend who forgot hers at home. The next stage (4) reflects a law and order orientation and is still centered on what society expects. Moral decisions are grounded in doing the right thing as defined by one's duties or obligations to society and others. In the *postconventional level,* morality is defined in terms of more abstract principles and values such as justice, equality, dignity, or respect. Individuals in this level question rules, laws, and societal mores in light of what is "right." Within the first stage (5) of postconventional morality, individuals consider various opinions, situations and values of different people before determining the morality of an action. They examine morality through the eyes of others. Individuals in this stage are committed to the social contract and to changing laws through democratic agreements. They are focused on the need to protect certain individual rights and settle disputes through agreed upon, negotiated or democratic processes. During the final stage of the postconventional level (6), morality is determined by universal ethical principles. Such moral decisions require impartiality. At this stage, a moral judgement may become innate and is grounded deeply in one's sense of what is universally right or wrong. Within stage 6, a commitment to justice may serve as the rationale for civil disobedience. Martin Luther King Jr., for example, argued that laws are only valid insofar as they are grounded in justice, and that a commitment to justice carries with it an obligation to disobey unjust laws. King also recognized, of course, the general need for laws and democratic processes (stages 4 and 5), and he was therefore willing to accept the penalties for his actions. Nevertheless, he believed that the higher principle of justice required civil disobedience (Kohlberg, 1981, p. 43).

4   Child Development and Dispositions

The connections between child and adolescent developmental theories and the need for responsive dispositions are clear. Developmental theory emphasizes the importance of students engaging in learning experiences where the adults are disposed to be challenging, empowering, facilitative, and connected. Teachers need to possess the necessary dispositions to make educational decisions that are reflective of theory and practice to be responsive to students' needs. Teachers also need to be disposed to guide students through moral development. Many technical dispositions align with lower levels of moral development with a focus on control, compliance, and following directions.

The teacher who is responsibly disposed to embrace and enact empowerment, connectedness, and creativity may better enable students to strive toward and exhibit glimpses of higher levels of moral development. Having the knowledge base and technical skills to address these various domains of child development is necessary, but is it sufficient, knowing that a teacher's dispositions affect choices that may significantly determine the effectiveness of reaching and teaching students? Content knowledge and understanding is replete with moral dilemmas. Ultimately, content knowledge is foundational to moral and ethical decisions made within various fields of knowledge that may directly affect our world. In Science, for example, how do we learn to navigate moral dimensions of pollutions? What are the moral and ethical decisions within the field of statistics when considering analysis choices and representations of data? Across and within various fields, content knowledge and skills are part of the bigger picture and challenges students will navigate beyond the world of school. Whether it is traversing differing conceptions of culture, class, ethnicity and justice within the Social Studies curriculum or the impact of literature and media as a reflection of or impetus for change in society, the intertwining of content understanding and morals cannot be ignored. Technically disposed teachers do not acknowledge this challenge, while responsive teachers embrace it.

Think again:

1 What further explicit linkages between responsive dispositions and specific developmental theories can you make?
2 How do you see teacher dispositions in relation to student developmental needs and characteristics? Can you give an example using a specific *Disposition in Action*?

3 What is the relationship between moral development and a teacher's dispositions in the classroom?

References

American Montessori Society. (2017). *Oh no! Things don't seem to be stacking up quite right!* Retrieved June 11, 2017, from https://amshq.org/Montessori-Education/ Introduction-to-MontessoriArnett

Arnett, J. J. (1999). Adolescent storm and stress, reconsidered. *American Psychologist, 54*(5), 317.

Bredekamp, S. (1987). *NAEYC position statement on developmentally appropriate practice in programs for 4-and 5-year olds.* Washington, DC: National Association for the Education of Young Children.

Checkley, K. (2004). Meeting the needs of the adolescent learner. *Education Update: ASCD, 46*(5). Retrieved from http://www.ascd.org/ASCD/pdf/journals/ed_update/ eu200408_checkley.pdf

Copple, C., & Bredekamp, S. (Eds.). (2009). *Developmentally appropriate practice in early childhood programs serving children from birth through age 8* (3rd ed.). Washington, DC: NAEYC.

Crain, W. (2015). *Theories of development: Concepts and applications.* London & New York, NY: Psychology Press.

Davidson, J. I. F. (1998). Language and play. In D. P. Fromberg & D. Bergen (Eds.), *Play from birth to twelve and beyond: Contexts, perspectives and meanings.* New York, NY: Garland Pub.

Hall, G. S. (1904). *Adolescence.* New York, NY: Appleton.

Kohlberg, L. (1981). *Essays on moral development: The philosophy of moral development.* San Francisco, CA: Harper & Row.

Montessori, M. (2013). *The Montessori method.* Piscataway, NJ: Transaction publishers.

Nichols, S. L. (2009). Adolescence. In E. M. Anderman & L. H. Anderman (Eds.), *Psychology of classroom learning: An encyclopedia* (Vol. 1, pp. 19–24). Farmington Hills, MI: Macmillan Reference, Gale.

Nichols, S. L., & Good, T. L. (2004). *America's teenagers – Myths and realities: Media images, schooling, and the social costs of careless indifference.* New York, NY: Routledge.

National Middle School Association. (2010). *This we believe: Keys to educating young adolescents.* Westerville, OH: National Middle School Association.

Open Education – The classroom, philosophical underpinnings, english beginnings. The american experience, controversies questions and criticisms. (2017). Retrieved August 23, 2017, from http://education.stateuniversity.com/pages/2303/Open-Education.html

Piaget, J. (1964). Part I: Cognitive development in children: Piaget development and learning. *Journal of Research in Science Teaching, 2*(3), 176–186.

Vygotsky, L. S. (1980). *Mind in society: The development of higher psychological processes.* Cambridge, MA: Harvard University Press.

Wadsworth, B. J. (1996). *Piaget's theory of cognitive and affective development: Foundations of constructivism.* White Plains, NY: Longman Publishing.

Wormeli, R. (2009). *Living with and teaching young adolescents: A teacher's perspective.* Retrieved August 31, 2017, from http://www.nmsa.org

CHAPTER 5

Why Dispositions? Why Now?

Think about:

1 What types of dispositions do you notice in the media?
2 What types of dispositions will be helpful or necessary in our future world?

• • •

We have been examining the concept of *Dispositions in Action* in light of the broader field of educator disposition research, developmental theory and posing the question, can DIA help us look at and intentionally develop teacher quality anew within the current educational context. However, the need to consider DIA at this time is related to more than the current educational context. Multiple real world challenges and changes in thinking about learning can be interwoven into the larger tapestry of *Dispositions in Action* to help us understand a bigger picture and reveal why we need to teach DIA, and why is now the time.

1   Dispositions and the 21st Century

The world is changing. In order to be happy and successful individuals, people need to not only adapt to this change but to embrace and lead it. We are moving into a time where information is at people's fingertips. If you don't know or understand something, you can Google it or ask Cortana. If we want our students to be more than consumers of information who blindly accept whatever they see on the Internet or in the media, we need to help them think differently. The reality of the 21st century, according to Zhao (2016), is that people will act as entrepreneurs and creators while finding ways to enhance human traits. This type of creative and entrepreneurial thinking is not cultivated through memorization, basic application, and unintentional collaboration in the classroom. Most of the knowledge and goods and services of in our students' future adult world do not yet exist. How do you prepare students for a world that is so rapidly evolving and changing? By teaching them to think. Teachers who are disposed to cultivating meaningful learning are best preparing 21st century citizens who will be able to guide and direct change rather than consume and react to it.

© KONINKLIJKE BRILL NV, LEIDEN, 2018 | DOI 10.1163/9789004364486_005

The 21st century has also seen an increase in virtual schooling, not only at the college level, but also for students pre-kindergarten through 12th grade. Digital learning is a growing trend among K-12 students nationwide with 2.7 million students across the United States taking part. In addition, there is an increasing number of students taught online through full-time online public school options. There is an 80% increase in the number of students attending school online and a 50% increase in the number of districts offering online or blended school settings. The number of full-time online public schools increased from 200,000 students to 315,000 students during the 2013–2014 school year (Gemin, Pape, Vashaw, & Watson, 2015). Some virtual schools are free to students as part of the public school system, while others are privatized profit-generating initiatives. The number of K-12 students attending school online continues to increase.

When analyzing the concept of online schools for children, the concept of *Dispositions in Action* may be applied. We could say that the need for an online "teacher" to be responsibly disposed may be limited. The majority of online courses focus on practice, memorization, finding correct answers, and feedback related to step-by-step processes aimed at improving student success. The online school is technically managed through the instructional design and user interface. There is little limited room for creativity in terms of assessing and evidencing content knowledge and understanding. An individual student's related curiosities and questions about what is being learned are not easily discussed and supported by the "teacher." Online education, too, is trying to become more responsive. Building options for creativity to meet a student's needs, such as engaging in peer forms and discussion posts, the use of videos, web conferencing, virtual reality and live streaming of classroom instruction could enable online teacher development programs to become more responsive in terms of DIA. Though there are efforts for online education to establish relationships with the students, the very human and critical thinking orientation of responsive dispositions is not easily replicated online. The foundations of *Dispositions in Actions*, relationships, are very different in face-to-face classrooms as compared to online learning environments. Computers may easily replace teachers when learning aligns with only the technical aspects of teaching. If relationships, discourse, and constructing knowledge with students is primary, perhaps teachers cannot be replaced so easily.

2   Dispositions and Emotional Intelligence

Society is changing. In order to be a happy and successful individual one must be more than intelligent. An individual may be smart, skilled, and motivated, but if they are working, interacting, or living with other people they need to know how to do that skillfully. We need to reexamine how we define intelligence. An essential part of intelligence is often neglected unless teachers are disposed to address it, namely emotional intelligence. According to Mayer, Salovey, and Caruso (2008), Emotional Intelligence (EI) includes the ability to engage in sophisticated information processing about one's own and others' emotions, and the use of this ability to guide one's thinking and behavior. Individuals with a high EI pay attention to, use, understand, and manage emotions. These skills serve adaptive functions for students that potentially benefit themselves and others. Initially, psychologists began to write and think about intelligence in terms of cognitive aspects, such as memory, reasoning and problem solving. However, some researchers recognized the importance of non-cognitive aspects. These aspects were referred to as "non-intellective" and were considered essential when predicting one's ability to succeed in life (Wechsler, 1940). Salovey and Mayer's (1990) research on emotional intelligence moved the concept forward by establishing a conceptual synthesis of a broad range of scientific findings, drawing together what had been separate strands of research. This synthesis includes not only their theory, but also other scientific developments related to emotional intelligence, such as the first studies of the emerging field of affective neuroscience, which explores how emotions are regulated in the brain (Goleman, 1995). Salovey and Mayer (1990) first used the term emotional intelligence to indicate a form of social intelligence that involves the ability to monitor one's own and other's' feelings and emotions, to discriminate among them, and to use this information to guide one's thinking and action. Building on this synthesis, Goleman (1995) authored a book called *Emotional Intelligence*, which became popular in its use, especially in corporate America.

The benefits and impact of teaching what is now termed social emotional intelligence (SEL) are far reaching. It supports children's development of neural circuitry, particularly the executive functions of the prefrontal cortex, which manages working memory and inhibits disruptive emotional impulses. The work of Greenberg, Kusche, and Cook (1995) reports that an SEL based curriculum not only boosts academic achievement but, even more significantly, much of the increased learning can result in improvements in attention and working memory, key functions of the prefrontal cortex. SEL can enhance children's learning while preventing problems such as violence. Helping children improve their self-awareness and confidence, manage their disturbing emotions and impulses, and increase their empathy pays off not just in improved behavior but in measurable academic achievement (Jennings & Greenberg, 2009). The data from a meta-analysis completed Roger Weissberg, the director of the Collaborative for Academic, Social and Emotional Learning at the University of Illinois at Chicago, analyzing 668 evaluation studies of SEL programs show that SEL programs yield a strong benefit in academic accomplishment, as demonstrated in achievement test results and grade-point averages. The meta analysis found that up to 50 percent of children showed improved achievement scores and up to 38 percent improved their grade-point averages. The programs also had a positive impact on behavior as misbehavior dropped by an average of 28 percent; suspensions by 44 percent; and other disciplinary actions by 27 percent. Attendance rates also rose and 63 percent of students demonstrated significantly more positive behavior.

We cringe at the sight of children fighting each other on YouTube. We wonder why there's so much gun violence and conflict among neighbors. We are dismayed at cyber bullying, racism, sexism and the overall lack of respect for self and others. We ask, "How can a young adolescent boy become a school shooter?" "Why are there so many suicides and drug overdoses among our youth?" We wonder why young people turn to gangs and terrorism as mistrust grows between citizens and police, parents and children, teachers and students, liberals and conservatives. In order for people to get along in an increasingly diverse society, they need to realize and develop emotional intelligence. Recent research indicates that we can do this. It just needs to be embraced and cultivated by teachers who are disposed to do so.

3   Dispositions and Mindfulness

Individuals are changing. In order to be happy and successful individuals people must be able to examine and understand the relationship between one's thoughts and reality. Instead of just existing in a melee of visual, auditory and virtual images, bombarded by information and entertainment, people need to be mindful of their experiences. Mindfulness is the basic human ability to be present and aware of where we are and what we are doing, while not becoming overly reactive or overwhelmed by what is going on around us. According to Kabat-Zinn (2009), mindfulness means paying attention in a particular way: on purpose, in the present moment, and without judgement.

The effect of teaching children to develop mindfulness has been documented to help students to reduce anxiety (Semple, Reid, & Miller, 2005), help students with behavior disorders to manage their aggressive behaviors (Singh et al., 2007), significantly decrease the impact of ADHD on learning (Zylowska et al., 2008), and overall enable children to deal with distressing life situations in more positive and productive ways.

The increased focus on consciousness of the mind has also led to the development of the growth mindset concept. Dweck (2006) believes that either we basically have a fixed-mindset, which implies that we believe our attributes and abilities are inherently fixed and unchanging, or a growth-mindset where we believe our talents and abilities can be improved and developed. She further suggests that one's mindset shapes our attitude so significantly that it is the ultimate factor that determines our success or failure. Research has indicated that students who believe their personal characteristics can be developed have less aggressive tendencies, and experience peer pressure with less stress (Zolfagharifard, 2015). Growth mindset can also increase academic performance (Yeager & Dweck, 2012). Unlike a fixed mindset, which implies intelligence is unchangeable, a growth mindset causes students to perceive the difficulties they face as something they can overcome, as opposed to feeling like there is no hope and that something might must be wrong with their intellectual abilities that cannot be fixed. Students become more inclined to grapple with difficult ideas, take risks in their learning, and accept and learn from failure. Teachers who are disposed to this way of thinking may best recognize and cultivate it in their instructional design and classroom culture, thus benefiting the social interaction and academic learning of the children they teach.

4 Dispositions and Democracy

Our democracy is changing. There appears to be an increasing divide between political parties, social classes, ethnic groups, religious beliefs and people in general. In order to have a voice in the world and at the same time act in the best interests of others, democratic thinking needs to be taught rather than assumed. Teaching democracy is far more than learning about governmental structures and voting practices and even the history of our country's journey into and through democracy. Democratic education is learning about democracy by living in one. Institutional structures that give young people the opportunity to participate in decision-making about meaningful issues can have an impact on their sense of responsibility, their ability to take a collective perspective, their prosocial behavior, their understanding of democratic values and processes, and their personal and political efficacy (Apple, 2009). A participatory and democratic school culture makes a significant difference in the foundational development of social responsibility (Berman, 1997). The current educational culture found in most schools is built upon a philosophy of scientific management. Hierarchy, linearity, efficiency, and competition are the norms. Approaches to teaching that evidence this type of philosophy are teacher-centered where the teacher acts as the "expert" with knowledge to impart to the students who act as passive recipients. Students begin to learn about their roles in the classroom and transfer that knowledge to society at large. If student roles are to be passive, non-questioning, centered on self-success, and dependent on an expert to think for them, this is problematic to our future democracy. This is complicated by the current "deskilling" and fragmentation of the curriculum, leading to instruction that replaces higher-order critical thinking and exploration of essential questions with learning isolated facts and decontextualized skills (Apple, 1981). According to Apple (2014), "Caring and connectedness, a sense of mutuality, trust and respect, and a freedom to challenge others, as well as a commitment to challenge the existing politics of official knowledge whenever and wherever it is repressive, [could] be rebuilt and maintained" (p. 160).

The current struggles of our democracy to maintain or redefine itself and work towards collective goals benefiting all should not be surprising. Why would we expect adults to get along without cultivating empathy? Why would we expect adults to listen to each other if they see no value in the "other"? Why would they know how to negotiate, compromise, and look beyond one's self, if they never had those experiences growing up? How can we learn to work together for common good if there is no shared concept of good? We need to move beyond an individualistic and narrow definition of a democratic society. Teachers who are disposed to building relationships through authentic interactions with and among students can help to lay the foundation for democracy that may actually ensure justice for all. The schools that best teach how to participate actively in democracy are schools that reflect democratic principles not only in word, but also in deed.

5   Dispositions and the Teacher Shortage

Teaching is changing. An increasing number of teachers are leaving the classroom and the profession. The leading cause of the current shortage is attrition rates among teachers, which account for as much as 95 percent of the entire educator drought. The US attrition rate is 8 percent annually, which is twice as high as rates in countries like Finland and Singapore (Camera, 2016). The impact of teacher retirement is relatively minor when compared to the number of teachers leaving due to other factors, such as job dissatisfaction or pursuit of other jobs. In fact, school staffing problems are not principally due to teacher shortages or from an insufficient supply of qualified teachers, but from an excess demand. The number of underprepared teachers who leave is even higher. The data indicate that a revolving door exists, that large numbers of qualified teachers are departing their jobs for reasons other than retirement (Ingersoll, 2002). The teaching force is "a leaky bucket, losing hundreds of thousands of teachers each year—the majority of them before retirement age," (Sutcher, Darling-Hammond, & Carver-Thomas, 2016). Overall, teachers and researchers say educators want more voice in school policies and plans. Many feel left out of key discussions and decisions.

Efforts to retain teachers have focused on salaries, benefits and alternative means of licensure to bring more people into the classroom. A decision to leave a profession that you entered because of caring, commitment, and the desire to make a difference in the world does not come easily. And some of the best teachers leave. They find themselves in an educational reality that runs counter to what they know and who they are inside. People who are disposed to be challenging, creative, connected and focused on empowerment of themselves and their students are in a place focused on completion, repetition, standardization and efficiency at the cost of students. Teachers leave because they have no voice or decision-making power and often feel required to do things they know are not best for their students and learning. There is a mismatch between their dispositions, who they are inside and how they think about the world, and the contrived, reductionist world of schooling. This is why teachers leave.

Teacher leadership and opportunities for teachers to have a voice in their profession and thus affect real change is the part of the solution to the shortage. Teaching has long struggled to become regarded as a real profession. This challenge goes back to the fact that the vast majority of teachers have been, and still continue to be women. The development of the National Board for Professional Teaching Standards was a response to this lack of professionalization, but has not reached the potential that it was hoped it would. Compounding this is the current political emphasis on cutting funding to public schools and institutions of higher learning who seek to prepare teachers as professionals and the devaluing of public education overall. In response to the teacher shortage, licensure requirements have been removed or minimized in many states, again, leading to fewer teachers entering the classroom who have the professional knowledge base and dispositions needed to be successful. Teachers who are disposed to think about their professional role as being one of leadership, establishing an impetus for change and challenging the status quo when it conflicts with what is best for students, are needed in these leadership roles.

6   Dispositions and the Testing Industry/Culture

The latest wave of educational improvement and reform has been branded as accountability to assure student success. The brand is supported by claimed goals such as making sure that no child is left behind, that learning gaps between different sets of students are erased, and that all students are college ready or even leave high school with a two-year college degree. The branding of the current school reform movement and related political mandates and legislative support is not coincidental, nor is it new. The No Child Left Behind Act clearly exhibits the relationship between the mandated accountability movement and the testing industry. Prior to this, Bill Clinton's Improving America's Schools act required states to take six tests in total. Under NCLB schools were required to make students take 14 tests total. The $5 million competitive Race to the Top grant program initiated under the Obama administration further intensified the testing frenzy (Figueroa, 2013). Many districts required even more tests. Schools hit hard by the economic recession and needing federal funding raced to improve their test scores to evidence their success and obtain the related monetary reward.

The testing industry, in particular corporations such as Pearson, stands to make millions of dollars in profit from testing mandates and related products that prepare students for these tests. Pearson Harris partnered with 18 states in the U.S., as well as Washington, D.C. and Puerto Rico in developing and providing statewide accountability tests within the public schools. As states began to adopt common core standards in English and Mathematics, Pearson's testing machine was not far behind as it created the PARCC test to align with these new standards. Pearson's testing dominance is not just within the world of K-12 schools, where it holds multimillion-dollar contracts with states, but also reaches to the higher education field in teacher preparation where its EdTPA is increasingly required by states for teacher licensure. CTB/McGraw-Hill is probably Pearson's main competitor, with several states across the country using its standardized tests. CTB/McGraw, with revenues of more than $2 billion, is best known for its TerraNova and California Achievement Tests. Other players include Education Testing Services, as well as Riverside Publishing and its parent company Houghton Mifflin Harcourt. Pearson has also jumped on the for-profit virtual charter school bandwagon, as it owns the Connections Academy, a company that runs for-profit, virtual charter schools (Figueroa, 2013).

Goals that may have been originally well intended and worthy aimed at enabling students to meet high standards, have been reduced to a standardized and profit driven definition of curricula, pedagogy, and assessment. The concept of educational standards should not be equated with this standardization, but often is. The concept of standards implies quality-learning experiences for all students and providing opportunities and approaches for all students to meet the standards. Embracing standards implies that teachers and schools need to have the flexibility to design curriculum, instruction, and learning environments that meet a variety of individual students needs and value the cultural, personal, developmental, and individual assets that each student brings to the classroom. Such an approach requires that learning is differentiated and that teachers have the skills and support to do this within their classrooms. If all students' needs are to be met, not all classrooms will look the same. Not all student assignments would be the same. Not all students would move to the next grade level at the same time. Grades would not be the foundation of daily assessment of learning and standardized test scores would not be the indicator of learning success. According to Kohn (2011), grades diminish student interest and learning, create a preference for the easiest possible task, and reduce the quality of student thinking. Grades are defined by their use as necessarily subjective, measuring multiple factors beyond student learning such as work ethic and effort, as they connote subjectivity by consensus. Coincidentally, grades and standardized tests tend to measure the kind of learning that does not matter (Kohn, 2000).

The push to move ahead quickly, be efficient, and provide measurable, numeric, "objective" data to prove teachers and schools are doing their jobs is pervasive in what passes for current educational improvement and reform. This focus on state mandates and prescriptive curricula, which is driven by the standardized testing movement, results in often-unarticulated consequences. These include a narrowing of the curriculum, pressure to cover testing content, and teaching that provides information as often isolated and disconnected facts and concepts. Testing dictates the use of time and schools as teachers work to not only meet end of grade test timelines, but also administer benchmark and practice tests throughout the school year. Teachers find themselves acting more as technicians following prompts, pacing guides and pre-packaged materials, rather than relying on their professional education, expertise and instincts. The goal of helping students to learn not only information, but also deeper content and contextual understanding and how this relates to the real world is clouded by this ethos of data collection and results producing. The importance of being a positive member of the school society today and of our future democratic society may be lost in the race to succeed. The belief that technical "how to" knowledge is sufficient for producing teacher excellence is a false belief (Collinson, 1999) that is being perpetuated by these accountability movements as they limit what teachers can do as decision-makers and learning designers. Related proposals for educational "reform" such as vouchers that provide public funding to charter school management companies, under the guise of parent empowerment through school choice, actually exacerbate inequalities (Frankenberg, Siegel-Hawley, & Wang, 2011). Such initiatives may cause us both to misrecognize what actually produces difficult social and educational problems and perhaps to miss some important democratic alternatives that may offer more hope in the long run (Beane & Apple, 1999).

The need for teachers who are professionally disposed to embrace professional inquiry to challenge limiting, hierarchical structures and mandates is greater within our standardized culture of schooling. According to the *Dispositions in Action* construct, technical dispositions align well with the standardized movement, but the definition of learning which results from technical discourse and practices is not aligned with the critical, democratic, thinking that is crucial to students' future success and the success of our future society. Teachers possessing responsive dispositions are better prepared to take on the standardized accountability based branding of education and work towards designing learning environments, instruction, and evaluation that are meaningful in light of students' needs to be successful beyond these limited measures and moreover, successful in the real world.

7   Dispositions and Devaluing of Teacher Education

Recent trends in funding of higher education and changes in certification requirements for teacher licensure may indicate a questioning of the worth of teacher education. The teacher shortage within many states has led to efforts to fast-track preparation for individuals to quickly and easily attain a license. The value of approaches to teacher preparation in which individuals may have no educational or pedagogical knowledge base, such as Teach for America, is increasing as we seek to get warm bodies into classrooms and misunderstand the complexities of teaching and learning beyond content transmission. The increase in movements towards charter schools, which may not require their teachers to have professional preparation and licensure, as well as the prevalence of temporary licenses coupled with multiple definitions of alternative routes to licensure are also problematic. The addition of for-profit charter schools, online K-12 schools, and online professional preparation being defined as completing tasks to earn competency badges, also begs for increased questioning and probing. In contrast to the efforts that may reduce the depth and effectiveness of preparation, we know that teachers make the biggest difference student learning (Darling-Hammond, Wei, & Johnson, 2009). We further know that teacher certification and professional preparation matters to the quality of teaching and learning in the classroom (Wilson, Floden, & Ferrini-Mundy, 2002). We also know there is a mass exodus of teachers leaving classrooms and that non-certified lateral entry teachers leave the profession at a rate 79 percent greater than other teachers do (Stancill, 2017). Despite what we know, such new approaches to acquire classroom teachers will continue, given the challenges teachers and schools face. So, this acquisition of teachers must be done well. Finding individuals who possess the right kind of dispositions, responsive dispositions, to hire and professionally develop may enable schools hiring from this eclectic pool of applicants to better assure quality learning in the classroom. Responsibly disposed teachers will develop meaningful relationships with and empower students as they engage them in the higher-level and critical thinking needed in today's world.

8   Dispositions and the Need for Higher Level Thinking

There is a connection between students' depth of content understanding and their teachers' dispositions. *Dispositions in Actions* studies have analyzed the nature of student learning within multiple classrooms, over time. Both formal and informal measures were used such as the evaluation of student work samples and products with the SOLO taxonomy to evaluate depth of student understanding, analysis of the types of discourse within classroom discussions and student conferencing, and interview data from teachers and their students. These measures revealed that higher levels of responsive teacher dispositions result in deeper student understanding and increased complex thinking. This is especially true at the higher ends of the range, where a level 3 (all responsive dispositions) correlated with extended abstract thinking and a level 1 (all technical dispositions) correlated with one-dimensional thinking. As a teacher's disposition to be responsive increases, an increasing number of connections within the content matter are made to create conceptual understanding and connections to the real world beyond school. Student understanding moves beyond a concrete level as students begin to grapple with abstract concepts that comprise our society and belief systems, such as productivity, justice, equity, and empathy.

It is incumbent upon educators to see that the educational experience is one that encourages students to think, to evaluate and to decide. In order for democracy to work, for students to become contributing members of an increasingly complex and diverse society, they must possess not only the basic knowledge and skills represented in standardized testing, but also the ability to think in deeper ways that are representative of what an educated democratic citizen should be like and able to do. They must be able to move beyond the surface level of unistructural thinking. Democracy in schools must be concerned with gathering and weighing evidence to determine good reasons to believe in something and efforts to understand other's perspectives. These are things that we rightfully expect an educated person to do (Levin, 1998). These goals reach far beyond those that can be measured by standardized testing.

9   Dispositions and Media Literacy

The impact of our rapidly progressing technical society and the ensuing bombardment of individuals with multiple messages from multiple media sources cannot be ignored. Instant access to information has changed the way we interact each other and with our world. Critical consumption of media and developing the necessary media literacy skills to make sense of this new world should be a foundational aspect of education. Without the ability to decipher and critique messages within and across multimedia sources, especially as related to use of the Internet and social media, people accept everything they see as legitimate, accurate, and truthful. The fact is this is just not the case.

Technically disposed teachers evidence discourse and behaviors that may reinforce limitations when investigating and interpreting messages. If one is disposed to be assuming and accepting of information and focused on following directives and compliance, this is modeled for students in the classroom. These dispositional tendencies run counter to the need for students to become media literate in meaningful and critical ways. It may also limit their creativity in becoming creators of knowledge rather than passive consumers.

10   Responsive Dispositions Now

Navigating the current contextual realities of the world in which we live is not a simple task. In order to be productive, successful, and happy in our 21st century reality, students need to become mindful of their own experiences, thoughts and feelings. They need to develop the emotional intelligence needed to live in an increasingly diverse and sometimes divisive world. Educational issues such as the teacher shortage, the testing industry, and the changing if not devaluing attitude towards teacher preparation, teachers, and schooling, compound the need to renegotiate and reimagine what learning means. Higher-level thinking skills that enable individuals to make connections between themselves, others, and understanding of their world are important as individuals navigate the evolution of our democratic society. Embracing new forms of communication and connection through informed and thoughtful media literacy can help these media to become assets and meaningful challenges for students in their lives now and in the future. Teachers that are disposed to respond to their students' questions, needs and their interactions with world around them are perhaps more important now than ever before.

Think again:

1 Which of the above sections on *Dispositions and* (21st century challenges, developing emotional intelligence, the need for mindfulness, our changing democracy, the teacher shortage, the testing industry, the devaluing of teacher education, the need for higher-level thinking, media literacy) do you consider most important? Why?
2 Do the issues examined within this chapter seem straightforward and readily accepted, or potentially controversial?
3 Rank order these issues: 21st century challenges, developing emotional intelligence, the need for mindfulness, our changing democracy, the teacher shortage, the testing industry, the devaluing of teacher education, the need for higher level thinking, media literacy) in terms of importance to you. Then rank order them to indicate which are most challenging to address. Discuss why.

References

Apple, M. W. (1981). Curricular form and the logic of technical control. *Economic and Industrial Democracy, 2*(3), 293–319.

Apple, M. W. (2009). Can critical education interrupt the right? *Discourse: Studies in the Cultural Politics of Education, 30*(3), 239–251.

Apple, M. W. (2014). *Official knowledge: Democratic education in a conservative age.* London: Routledge.

Beane, J. A., & Apple, M. W. (1999). *Democratic schools: Lessons from the chalk face.* Buckingham: Open University Press.

Berman, S. (1997). Civil society and political institutionalization. *American Behavioral Scientist, 40*(5), 562–574.

Camera, L. (2016). *The teacher shortage crisis is here.* Retrieved August 29, 2017, from https://www.usnews.com/news/articles/2016-09-14/the-teacher-shortage-crisis-is-here

Collinson, V. (1999). Redefining teacher excellence. *Theory Into Practice, 38*(1), 4–11.

Darling-Hammond, L., Wei, R. C., & Johnson, C. M. (2009). Teacher preparation and teacher learning: A changing policy landscape. In G. Sykes, B. L. Schneider, & D. N. Plank (Eds.), *Handbook of education policy research* (pp. 613–636). New York, NY: Routledge.

Dweck, C. S. (2006). *Mindset: The new psychology of success.* New York, NY: Random House.

Figueroa, A. (2013). *8 things you should know about corporations like Pearson that make huge profits from standardized tests*. Retrieved August 23, 2017, from http://www.alternet.org/education/corporations-profit-standardized-tests

Frankenberg, E., Siegel-Hawley, G., & Wang, J. (2011, January 10). Choice without equity: Charter school segregation. *Education Policy Analysis Archives/Archivos Analíticos de Políticas Educativas, 19*(1), 1–96. Retrieved from https://doi.org/10.14507/epaa.v19n1.2011

Gemin, B., Pape, L., Vashaw, L., & Watson, J. (2015). *Keeping pace with K-12 digital learning: An annual review of policy and practice*. Durango, CO: Evergreen Education Group.

Goleman, D. P. (1995). *Emotional intelligence: Why it can matter more than IQ for character, health and lifelong achievement*. New York, NY: Bantam Books.

Greenberg, M. T., Kusche, C. A., Cook, E. T., & Quamma, J. P. (1995). Promoting emotional competence in school-aged children: The effects of the PATHS curriculum. *Development and Psychopathology, 7*(1), 117–136.

Ingersoll, R. M. (2002). The teacher shortage: A case of wrong diagnosis and wrong prescription. *NASSP Bulletin, 86*(631), 16–31.

Jennings, P. A., & Greenberg, M. T. (2009). The prosocial classroom: Teacher social and emotional competence in relation to student and classroom outcomes. *Review of Educational Research, 79*(1), 491–525.

Kabat-Zinn, J. (2009). *Wherever you go, there you are: Mindfulness meditation in everyday life*. New York, NY: Hachette Books.

Kohn, A. (2000). *The case against standardized testing: Raising the scores, ruining the schools*. Portsmouth, NH: Heinemann.

Kohn, A. (2011). The case against grades. *Educational Leadership, 69*(3), 28–33.

Levin, B. (1998). An epidemic of education policy: (What) can we learn from each other? *Comparative Education, 34*(2), 131–141.

Mayer, J. D., Salovey, P., & Caruso, D. R. (2008). Emotional intelligence: New ability or eclectic traits? *American Psychologist, 63*(6), 503.

Salovey, P., & Mayer, J. D. (1990). Emotional intelligence. *Imagination, Cognition and Personality, 9*(3), 185–211.

Semple, R. J., Reid, E. F., & Miller, L. (2005). Treating anxiety with mindfulness: An open trial of mindfulness training for anxious children. *Journal of Cognitive Psychotherapy, 19*(4), 379–392.

Singh, N. N., Lancioni, G. E., Singh Joy, S. D., Winton, A. S., Sabaawi, M., Wahler, R. G., & Singh, J. (2007). Adolescents with conduct disorder can be mindful of their aggressive behavior. *Journal of Emotional and Behavioral Disorders, 15*(1), 56–63.

Stancill, J. (2017). NCSU, UNC to offer online program for teacher licensure. *The News & Observer*. Retrieved March 15, 2017, from http://www.newsobserver.com/news/local/education/article131702269.html

Sutcher, L., Darling-Hammond, L., & Carver-Thomas, D. (2016). *A coming crisis in teaching? Teacher supply, demand, and shortages in the U.S.* Palo Alto, CA: Learning Policy Institute. Retrieved November 21, 2016, from https://learningpolicyinstitute.org/product/coming-crisis-teaching

Wechsler, D. (1940). Non-intellective factors in general intelligence. *Psychological Bulletin, 37,* 444–445.

Wilson, S. E., Floden, R. E., & Ferrini-Mundy, J. (2002). Teacher preparation research: An insider's view from the outside. *Journal of Teacher Education, 53*(3), 190–204.

Yeager, D. S., & Dweck, C. S. (2012). Mindsets that promote resilience: When students believe that personal characteristics can be developed. *Educational Psychologist, 47*(4), 302–314.

Zhao, Y. (2016). From deficiency to strength: Shifting the mindset about education inequality. *Journal of Social Issues, 72*(4), 716–735.

Zolfagharifard, R. (2015, February 8). *Growth-mindset vs fixed-mindset.* Retrieved August 28, 2017, from https://positivepsychologyprogram.com/growth-vs-fixed-mindset/

Zylowska, L., Ackerman, D. L., Yang, M. H., Futrell, J. L., Horton, N. L., Hale, T. S., Pataki, C., & Smalley, S. L. (2008). Mindfulness meditation training in adults and adolescents with ADHD: A feasibility study. *Journal of Attention Disorders, 11*(6), 737–746.

PART 2

What Does It *Look Like? Responsive Dispositions in the Classroom*

∴

CHAPTER 6

Assessment: The Disposition to Be Critical and Challenging

by Lois Boone

If my future were determined just based upon the performance of a standardized test, I wouldn't be here. I guarantee you that.
MICHELLE OBAMA

Technically speaking... Good classroom assessment is efficient, clear, objective, and frequent. It is easy to distinguish right answers from wrong ones and to numerically calculate a student's level of learning or achievement. Good assessment is standardized to allow for comparison from student to student, teacher to teacher, school to school, and nation to nation. This is how we can tell if we are successful as teachers. This is how we hold students accountable. Technically speaking good classroom assessment is efficient, objective, and frequent.

In reality... Testing. State testing. Just the mention causes a flutter in the stomach. And this happens within the gut of an experienced teacher. Twenty-six years, to be exact. Why does this cause such angst? I am a content knowledgeable teacher. Technically speaking, my instruction is aligned with Common Core State Standards that are interwoven into lesson plans designed to meet and target necessary goals to be accomplished. My students provide data through a variety of resources: Reading Counts quizzes, Scholastic Inventory tests offered each quarter, county benchmarks offered three times a year, teacher-made multiple choice tests through various online testing resources such as Socrative and SchoolNet. My students and I set achievement goals. We sport our scores from last year's EOG's in our daily agenda as a reminder of how we will grow a minimum of seven scale score points from last year. Parent conferences are held, especially for those who possess a PEP (Personal Education Plan) folder, so that documentation of efficient classroom strategies can be addressed as measures offered to help increase EOG performance.

I have done all the expected actions prescribed to me. Test scores of my past should ease some of my anxiousness. But, alas, there is that pit-in-the-stomach-feeling as I write. No surprise, really. Our school is preparing for administering EOG's next week. I am reminded how my students must be feeling now. There certainly has been a rise of those all too familiar student behaviors, the ones

© KONINKLIJKE BRILL NV, LEIDEN, 2018 | DOI 10.1163/9789004364486_006

which indicate increased stress. It is normal and we are all in this together, I have told them. And what gets me through this is reflecting on the process of how I have assessed my students all year long. I have a sense of how each student will do through the various pieces of collected data. But more than anything, I have a sense of the confidence level each student will bring to these important tests, and it has not been through just drill, skill, and test processes. I know I have collected a variety of assessments, both formative and summative, to indicate acquisition of material and have tutored those who have needed extra reading assistance. As my anxiousness increases with these thoughts, I am comforted in the solid relationships at this point of the year with my students and feel a real bond with them. It's the kind of relationship that makes me feel sad at the reality that soon our paths will part as the year comes to a close. In the end, after 8th grade promotion night, I will hug the students good-bye, wish them a safe summer, and probably never once talk about the results of this test. But, to be in this place at this time with my students, and myself we have focused throughout the course of this year with a mission to grow academically, and we are feeling the pressure. Alas, Standardized Assessment is a necessary part of the process.

So, what all have I learned on this teaching journey regarding assessments? Authenticity. The best assessments allow students to create, generate, and apply skills acquired from instruction. The best assessments allow students to demonstrate critical thinking applied through written responses. These include projects, essays, short answer responses, or various other written reflections. The teacher who provides assessments that probe, focus on quality answers to demonstrate understanding of important criteria, and look for answers that demonstrate deep understanding, has what is called a Critical Disposition. These teachers often utilize a rubric stating clear objectives that allow for understanding of clear expectations and what is necessary for a successful outcome. The Critical Teacher utilizes means of evaluation for students that demonstrate deeper understanding of material and challenge student thinking.

Let's consider the multiple choice-type test. Students who are given these tests are restrained to determining the best of four provided options to consider which one is the best choice or the right answer. While easy to grade, these tests do not have students generating or creating answers. The answers are either right or wrong and produce grades based on bubbled accuracy. The teacher who is centered on completion of tasks, focused on accuracy of answers, and concerned with pumping many grades into the grade book, is in fact one who is identified as an Assuming teacher and tends to use this type of test most often. Using this type of testing as the only way to determine acquisition of material is in fact shortsighted. Including some form of written reflection, such as open-ended questions, truly provides a better understanding of whether a student "gets" the material. It has been my experience that limited response testing, which does not allow students to demonstrate application of acquired skills, sets up students for having to relearn material, and therefore inhibits the ability to succeed when the complexity level increases the following school year. The damage is that if all a test is doing is measuring success of the week's study, it has not contributed to long-term retention of information. Herein lies the concern for students who year after year are deemed successful or not based upon multiple choice-type testing. I think about past students who suffered from testing anxiety and a fear of failure. These were the students who brought their A-game to class daily. They were successful in varied approaches of determining acquisition of set skills, and they became more confident. However, as soon as a summative assessment was offered that was narrowed down to selecting the best answer choice, these were the students who exhibited testing anxiety and would be the last to finish in class as they were consumed with worry. I can attest to the increase of student anxiety throughout my years of teaching due to pressures of constant testing on the county level and state level. We should not kill the love of learning, but unfortunately, in some classrooms it is happening. Success is determined by these results when there are multiple ways to measure student achievement.

For example, a student I taught last year whose name I shall change to Micah. As I got to know Micah, who was in my AIG class, he was appropriately social and academically on par with his classmates. Throughout the course of the year, I began to notice Micah's testing patterns. He demonstrated creativity and mastery of varied class projects, but one thing disturbed me. As soon as an in-class test was given that was EOG-like in format, he would shut down. He would be the last to finish and hand in his work, at times with tears in his eyes. Initially this was quite perplexing because based upon other types of multiple-choice tests, such as Reading Counts, where he was reading above grade literature and was successful with the 10-question quizzes, this scene was not matching up. As we approached the spring of that year and best testing practices for this type of test were in process, Micah was not himself. I checked in with his other content teachers, and they were seeing good grades from him but a stressed student when testing. This was a flag to go back and review Micah's EOG history. When reviewed, this was a student who was not passing his EOG reading tests each year! The first time I read through my students EOG scores the connection to each student was not yet formed, therefore, this low score did not resonate like it did upon later review. I was floored! This was a capable, smart student with a passion for learning. This was the student who early in the year informed me that his goal in life was to be a middle school teacher. How exciting for a middle school teacher to hear! When the realization hit that his 8th grade EOG may be no different in result due to his extreme testing anxiety, I was so grateful to have a plethora of documented data and a portfolio of written assignments to prove why Micah needed to continue with his Honors track at the high school. This is a prime example of why it is so important to know and understand our students. I shudder to think that I would have limited my approaches to offering assessments which did not provide a comprehensive picture of each of my students and each one's ability to demonstrate higher order connections and deeper thinking.

I see all my students as being extraordinarily bright and highly creative. I believe in holding the bar high for all and adjusting as needed. Although reading achievement levels indicate the proficiency of each student, it is not intended to be melodramatic when I say I see them all starving for deep, rich, meaningful activities. All students benefit from opportunities to draw from their amazing ability to connect and produce creative projects that demonstrate acquisition of material regardless of reading capabilities. I have found students to quickly become bored at mundane multiple-choice assessments that keep responses at a surface level. The teacher that maintains a Challenging Disposition invites higher-level dialogue within student-generated products. These products pull the standards of Bloom's: Analyzing, Evaluating, and Creating, and align them with Common Core objectives to be sure my responsive teaching style is also laced with important technical features. These are important drivers in unit planning as the teacher with a Challenging disposition continues to challenge herself to bring the best to her students. The payoff is the quality of the assignments. While high flyers expect to make good grades, the Assuming Teacher can quickly fall into the natural trap that these students typically make A's. This brings to light the necessity of a rubric which validates the grade. Did the student truly demonstrate proficiency on required criterion? Also, on the rubric a teacher comment section needs to be present to allow a genuine response to the work. All students value teacher feedback, which should reflect positive attributes as well as constructive suggestions for improvement. It is meaningful and validating to students that his/her teacher takes the time to write a personal response to the work. Noting that grading time can be limited, I always communicate to my students that the "Mrs. Boone signature smiley face" indicates that if the student had been sitting with me at the moment I was grading his or her assignment, the exclamation, "Wow!" would have been heard. The feedback may be quick and simple, but it is so effective for those smaller assignments. If the work falls short of the rubric requirements in some manner, I am careful to remain positive yet point out some areas that needed improvement. Students value the time teachers take to reflect on submitted work. It provides that special dialogue moment between teacher and student, an especially difficult endeavor when class sizes are large.

As all teachers know, we wear multiple hats on any given day and moment. We are responsible role models in a position to develop meaningful relationships with our students. We provide a pathway and vision to help students achieve at levels they never dreamed possible. We cheerlead students to realize hidden potential. Assessment is one way to unleash the creative individual. We challenge, we stretch the mind, we do more than push grades, and we are certainly to keep expectations of students at levels which require more than they believe possible. For example, one project I gave this year was a courtroom simulation after reading Poe's "Tell-Tale Heart." The purpose was to determine if the narrator was guilty of precalculated murder or innocent by grounds of insanity. This assignment was differentiated for inclusion, regular, and AIG classes. A rubric was provided for each class. The outcome was phenomenal. From the lesson, not only did students have to cite text evidence for support via differentiated documentation, they had to *become* the position. A jury and judge were determined for each class, and the most convincing argument won. This assignment was referenced all year for the experience it provided, and many students learned they had a knack for debate. Future lawyers? Future leaders in some capacity? This assessment unleashed more than a grade; it was a 21st century focus for my 8th graders. They begged for more projects of this nature!

Which brings to mind, the necessity for differentiation of assessments. From the mainstreamed inclusion setting, standard classes, and AIG classes, assessments need to challenge all levels.

The 2015–2016 school year brought a need to differentiate more than ever as I taught students below grade level to students several years above grade level in my English Language Arts classes. The challenge for me was to create differentiated assessments for diverse literacy needs. For example, a curriculum focus for our school was for all grade levels to incorporate a Greek and Latin roots program. This included designated lists per grade level. I chose to keep the instructional lists the same for all classes. Assignments, however, were differentiated per class for independent practice. The students understood that my homework assignments were purposeful and meaningful. The activities were presented on a menu board, and classes were given options appropriate for their particular class to choose. These assignments were designed for multiple learning styles and included auditory, visual, technology, and writing goals. AIG students enjoyed the opportunity to choose to write stories with newly acquired vocabulary, some of which became ongoing sagas shared with the class. Some chose to create a skit involving classmates to enact the next day. My artistic students drew a picture inclusive of many of the words which inspired a story to share. My inclusion students and regular ed classes received the same menu but with modifications. Classes were given choice options accordingly. Some of these activities included creating a comic strip or writing an acrostic poem but again the objective was to create, generate, and be prepared to present. Seldom did a student come unprepared for class; this was just not an option. If this did happen, the student was held accountable to complete the work.

This leads me to the student who attempts to perform tasks in a minimalist manner. This student is satisfied with just getting by with assignments. A teacher who demonstrates an Accepting disposition will be content if the student gets the work in on time and complies with the rubric, even if it falls short of exemplary work. How many very bright students have you found to be this way? Funny how at times, too, this student can pass a multiple-choice test so easily. A test designed in such a manner does not require much effort, and the unmotivated student prefers this type of test. I'm sure we have all had the range of students from struggling to the brightest who can exhibit a lack of work ethic. As mentioned in the third paragraph, if we are not careful, our assessment scores may not reflect true acquisition of material and that can negatively impact our understanding of where students stand in terms of demonstrating academic growth. It reminds me of the limitations that reading quiz programs create. My goal each year is to journey with students in the rich studies of great literary works. Studying an author and evaluating the impact of his or her intended life message with students often causes me to pinch myself and boast, "Look what I get to do today! I get to read a great book and have in-depth dialogue with some pretty amazing young adults." Learning is so exciting and student feedback is so inspiring. To minimize such efforts with offering only a multiple-choice assessment is deflating. Using an engaging assessment allows for authentic responses generated by students and an overall bigger picture of student acquisition. It is so important to stay connected to what students really think and understand. A Responsive disposition within a teacher considers approaches which involve critical thinking, challenging engagement, and avoids assumptions and acceptance of mediocre effort. It is the student voice that continually offers inspiration, and in the busyness of our days, we really need to take note and listen.

As the writing of this section has been a work in progress, the school year has wrapped up, and state testing is completed. The final days of school were less stressful and the perfect time to ask my eighth grade students to provide feedback to the question: What qualities make a good teacher? I was impressed with their honesty. I immediately picked up on a common thread through the majority of reflections: having a relationship with the teacher. So many wanted the teacher to like her students, smile more, hold true and fair consistent classroom expectations and engage classes in fun learning activities. Of the ninety-six responses, not one mentioned EOG testing. Only two referenced testing in general at all.

Yes, I will offer assessments of a variety of kinds. Yes, I will review best test taking strategies as multiple choice exams are the debated means of establishing school performance and normed proficiency. But I will remember, as stated in their words, to listen to my students, design authentic, creative activities which allow for fun learning, and to maintain a disposition not of just Technical features of instruction (the Assuming and Accepting teacher) but of Responsive features (the Critical and Challenging teacher). I want to pay attention to *how* students learn best. Classrooms that are organized into being inviting, inspiring, and engaging, are classrooms where students of all abilities achieve greater confidence. With a desire to come to class, to be with teachers who want to be with them, and participating in mutual respect, students' grades tend to increase by true nature of this design.

Teaching energy has not waned for me, and retirement, although in my near future, is far away. I cannot imagine a more purposeful existence than my daily role as a classroom teacher. Each year I "adopt" about one hundred plus middle schoolers. They become "my kids," and our collective, positive classroom synergy makes goals attainable, assessments and all.

CHAPTER 7

Instruction: The Disposition to Be Facilitative
by Sarah Chapman

> I like a teacher who gives you something to take home to think about besides homework.
>
> LILY TOMLIN AS EDITH ANN

Technically speaking... A good teacher knows the curriculum, tells the students facts they need to know, and expect the students to follow directions to show they have learned the material. All teachers have a curriculum that we are expected to cover throughout the year. Such a curriculum often provides continuity in what students learn if they move to a different school or district. Historically, the content has been taught through lecture, assigned readings, solving pages of math problems, and testing the knowledge. My teachers in this manner directed much of my K-12 education. But do we have to continue teaching this way simply because it has always been that way? Change is a constant in life, so why should education stay the same? Right now, you can probably hear your mother saying, "It was good enough for me, so I don't know why we feel like we should change it now!"

In reality... Students do not have to sit at a desk and have the teacher lecture in order to learn, though this is how many people believe education should still work. A teacher with a facilitative disposition to instruction is able to explore the required curriculum and help students learn how to access and evaluate information while also guiding students' active learning. When students participate in learning activities that require inquiry and critical thinking skills, they make connections to real life as well as learn to work with peers to find answers.

One day as students worked in my classroom a few years ago, an intelligent and hardworking student said to me, "Mrs. Chapman, Social Studies is my least favorite subject." I was surprised to hear this because she was attentive during class and volunteered to participate more than most. When I asked her why, she said there was so much to remember and she couldn't remember it all, but she liked it better in my class because it was more fun and she felt like she learned more. I believe this is because I try to facilitate my students' learning rather than direct it.

Think back to when you were in school. What content do you remember learning? Do you remember what your class read round robin style in social

© KONINKLIJKE BRILL NV, LEIDEN, 2018 | DOI 10.1163/9789004364486_007

studies? I don't. But I do remember counting to figure out which paragraph I would read and practicing to myself until it was my turn. Do you remember formulas from the probability and statistics unit? I don't. But I remember working with a few of my classmates to investigate and figure out how probability works by analyzing the likelihood of winning the lottery. Do you remember the lectures on how to diagram sentences? I don't. But I do remember the day my 11th grade teacher wrote "I am." on the board, asked us if it was a complete sentence, and facilitated a heated discussion so we, as a class, could decide. My memorable educational moments are not of teachers directing my learning – they are of teachers building relationships and effectively facilitating it.

The current workforce requires individuals to collaborate and problem solve. If we as teachers only feed information to our students, they will not have the opportunities to learn how to think critically or work effectively with others. I would be doing my students a great disservice if I did not facilitate these opportunities for them. It's not always easy to teach in this way, but in the end, it is always rewarding when it's done well. In order to provide the most effective lessons and units for my students, I work hard to remember a few things:

> I don't have to teach the way I was taught. And sometimes I have to set my preferences aside.

I received a pretty good education when I was in school. It involved a lot of memorizing and repeating, but that was appropriate for the time. Many of the students who graduated from my high school in my small farming community planned to become a teacher, work in an auto factory, or farm. These careers require learning a process and producing an output, much like our education that was based on the factory system. As I previously mentioned, the workforce has changed. Many of our students will have jobs that don't even exist yet. We need to teach them to effectively and independently learn new systems and technology because they won't be in school forever. This can't happen with the old educational system.

I have a confession. I like it when students work silently and independently. There are many days when the factory-style education system is very tempting. This means students would read a passage or a chapter and write down their answers typically to recall level textbook questions. But are they getting the most out of this type of rote learning? Students learn more deeply about a topic if they can discuss it with others or participate in a hands-on activity.

I once had a principal who would often tell us at the end of a long day, "If you're not tired, you're not doing it right." Hearing this often aggravated me, mostly because I was tired, but at the same time, it encouraged me to keep doing what

I was doing. By the same token, you could tell your students "If I'm working harder than you are then you're not doing it right." Facilitative instruction puts the hard work and worthwhile results in the hands of the student. The hard work of the teacher is in designing instructional opportunities for students to actively learn rather than the teacher finding and memorizing information to tell the students and have them copy down as notes. The students do the learning and learning is engaging.

> *I don't have to know everything, but I do have to model how I figure things out.*

Students are curious. As I plan my lessons, one of my steps is anticipating what questions the students will ask. I get better every year, but they almost always have other questions. Most of the time, I can sufficiently answer their questions, but not always. In those cases, I say, "Hmm, I'm not sure, but we will figure it out." At the beginning of each year, students have a hard time understanding how I don't know an answer because I'm the teacher. This, however, helps my students see that none of us have all the answers, and I take the opportunity to show them how to find reliable information. Yes, there are days we are short on time or we are in a groove, so I'll tell the student who asked to do some research for homework (others will often volunteer to research as well) and make a note to follow up with the student(s) the next day. If I have time, I'll research as well so I can fill in interesting or important facts they may miss. What if they don't research it before the next class? Then we research it together. What does researching as a class look like? It does sound like it could take a while, but I try to keep it to five minutes or so. The first thing I do is open a new browser tab and project it on the screen. (If inappropriate content may pop up, I wait to project until I can get to a place where everything is okay for middle school eyes.) After I type our topic, I talk to them about each suggested site and why we will look at it or not. This helps them learn about reliable sources. As we look at and discuss the information from one or two reliable sites, I also point out the information we would use to cite our sources. Time permitting, we will create citations.

After I model the research process a few times, I begin asking them how to find the information and why. They don't even realize when I transition them to conducting the research on their own because we are focusing on information and ideas they want to know. To the students, we are just finding out about something they want to know about, but by using their interests, I am also guiding them to research and interpret what they find (and give credit to their sources) – two important skills needed for critical thinking.

It's okay to give students choices.

Student learning is the goal. How do we best learn? I believe that we all learn more when we are interested in what are doing. Most students will complete comprehension questions or fill out graphic organizers appropriately in order to get a good grade, but this doesn't mean that all of those students are truly ·learning the content. However, if students have choices in how they work with the content, they will be more likely to understand and retain the information. Giving students choices doesn't mean giving up control of the learning environment. By teaching and modeling expected behaviors and procedures, students will come to thrive in a learning environment that includes activities such as literature circles, projects with choice boards, writing workshops, and centers. The teacher is able to facilitate learning through this type of activity that encourage students to take responsibility and be active learners. Eventually your students know how to run the classroom and make learning happen. This frees up the teacher to interact more directly and one-on-one with students as they work and has the added benefit of assuring that the class will go on and students can learn when you are out for a workshop or not feeling well. Your sub plans usually look like "The students know what to do, so let them do it."

Last fall, two education students from our partnership university spent the day with my classes and me. I put them to work as soon as they walked in the door; this required them to conference with students about activities chosen from a menu board for the book project we were working on. They talked to students about what they chose, and I encouraged the teacher candidates to find out *why* they made those choices. During planning, they wanted to ask questions about what it is really like in the classroom. One asked about my philosophy of education. I immediately answered: building relationships is the most important thing I do in my classroom. They both looked surprised, and one of them said that had never considered that as a philosophy of education and asked me to explain.

I can't effectively teach a student until I have an understanding of him and he trusts me and feels safe. Once the relationships are built, I am able to better impact their learning. As we continued to discuss the day, I had them share what they had learned about some of the students in the short time they interacted with each other. I was able to use that to illustrate how well I got to know my students in the couple of months since school started. I work hard to get to know my students, and realizing this helped the teacher candidates understand why I did some of the things I did throughout the day, how I chose to be instructionally facilitative. I made intentional small decisions to continually facilitate students' learning. I:

- Gave one student a time limit so he wouldn't obsess over choosing the perfect activities (as I knew he would).
- Encouraged a student to choose a variety of activities to challenge herself rather than simply doing what is easiest.
- Emphasized that a student should choose what interests him rather than what his friends were doing.
- Listened to all of the students who were excited about ideas and plans they had, and pushed them to go deeper.
- Worked to engage the student who dreaded coming to school and often didn't.

All of this happened while students read, analyzed, discussed, and created because the relationships allowed me to facilitate this learning. Now that the school year is over, I know that book project was memorable for them because I heard students talking about it in June. I didn't hear any of them talking about notes they took or passages and comprehension questions they completed.

Collaboration makes a difference.

While collaboration doesn't happen in every activity every day, it is an important part of our students' education. They need to know how to work together for a common purpose, which should include problem solving and discussion of content. This takes teachers who are responsively disposed to cultivate collaboration. Our students need to find their voices and learn how to share ideas and opinions appropriately. It is exciting to see students, who are sure that they can't do an assignment, work together by building on each other's ideas and create products that illustrate their thoughtfulness and creativity. Because this is something they often haven't previously experienced, I model it for them by answering their questions with questions. Yes, this frustrates them, but I encourage and guide them to work with their partners to find answers. By doing this, the students are able to move from thinking there is an exact answer or way I want them to do the assignment, to working together to understand that their product can be what they want it to be as long as it addresses the purpose of the assignment (Rubric provided, of course).

Requiring students to collaborate also allows us to facilitate appropriate working relationships by pushing them to work with students with whom they wouldn't normally choose to work, valuing others who may think differently or have a different skill set and by teaching them conflict resolution when a problem arises. This isn't always easy because at the first sign of a problem, the students' instinct is often to want to work with someone else or tattle to the teacher. After I have taught my students the procedures and expectations of group work, I find that I do not spend as much of my time keeping students on task. They are focused because the choices keep them interested. This allows me to focus on students who may have trouble getting along with their partners and to help them figure out how to work through that. They know that kindness is always expected in our classroom, but it's not always easy for some of the students. I use these opportunities to help them learn to interact with others who may be difficult to get along with or who they haven't always gotten along with in the past. Honest conversations and high expectations are necessary. But this has allowed me to help students develop leadership skills over the years, even in those who are not typical student leaders.

Technology can be a great tool – when used effectively.

No matter what path our students take, we know that they will have to use technology throughout their lives. It is easy to assume that they know how to use everything available to them. I mean, when I can't get my classroom technology to work, I don't need to put in a tech request because my students can usually figure out what the problem is. If I can't get a student Chromebook to turn on because the power key is missing, no problem – at least one student will know what to do. They have, after all, been using computers and cell phones all their lives. They don't understand how I survived life before getting my first cell phone once I was out of college. However, when I ask them to send me an email with an appropriate subject line, most of my students have no idea what that means, and I get 50 emails with all of the content typed into the subject line instead of the body of the email.

We use computers a lot in my class, but I never expect that they know how to do what is necessary to complete assignments because many of them do not have computers at home. Even if they do have computers at home, I can't expect that they have done what I want them to do. However, there is so much technology out there to reinforce concepts we work with that allow students to work at their own pace. This means facilitating and collaboration. Helping students to find related materials and answer their questions about what they are investigating, using technology, teaches them important life skills and emphasizes lifelong learning. Working together with a partner to explore new ideas and think about different paths to understanding allows students to move at different paces and for differentiation to become a natural part of the process. Using technology has allowed my students to not only explore ideas, but to also find evidence to support those ideas. Through inquiry-based projects, my students can research and modify their ideas and find real world examples for support.

When using technology I do what I always do. I model what I expect, and then let them practice. Just setting them free on computers and then sitting at my desk isn't facilitating learning. That approach does not guide students to make good decisions about how and what to learn. I collaborate with them and monitor what they are doing so they can learn to do things such as create documents, conduct research, and appropriately participate in class discussion boards. Facilitating learning and collaborating using technology has also helped me build connections with students and provides another way to communicate and connect with them with them outside of the classroom.

Students have valid opinions, too.

At first, students often struggle with an instructionally facilitative teacher. I regularly request feedback from students about the lessons, projects, and activities that happen in my classroom. At the beginning of the year, many students tell me they don't like facilitated learning because "it is too hard" or "there's not enough information." Instead, they prefer teacher-led, whole class activities because they know what to expect and usually perform well on assignments. I could ignore their feelings on the matter and carry on full-force, but that won't do anything to change mindsets. If students feel their opinions are being heard, we can start building trust. If I know why a student resists a teaching technique I use, I can better educate that student. I continue a dialogue with the students who resist facilitated learning and find that the main reason they struggle with facilitated learning at the beginning of the school year is that they are pushed out of their comfort zone, whether it is because they have to grapple with information or collaborate in a way they haven't before. Because I talk with these students about their feelings, they are more and more willing to put effort into their assignments.

As the year goes on, students begin to look forward to facilitated and collaborative learning. Part of this is because they feel like they have a say in their learning. Part of this is because they begin to find value and interest in learning. I can tell when they start to appreciate these methods when their feedback for lessons and activities becomes more positive. Rather than hearing how hard the activities are, students focus on what they are getting out of the activities. Student comments indicate that they enjoy being guided through the learning process rather than the having the teacher always feed them information. They begin to look forward to true collaboration because everyone is included and has specific roles that they get to choose. They start realizing that when they are interested in what they are working on, they learn better and enjoy the experience more. And in my eyes, the best feedback is when I get comments similar to this... "During this book project, I felt more confident while I worked. Even when I didn't understand something, I knew that I could talk to you for you to give me feedback and guide me in the right direction because you listen to my ideas. This is the first time I liked everything about a project. I think I learned a lot more too."

CHAPTER 8

Instruction: The Disposition to Be Creative
by Jessi Hall

> Tell me and I forget. Teach me and I remember. Involve me and I learn.
>
> BENJAMIN FRANKLIN

Techincally speaking... A good teacher discovers and uses a way to explain concepts and illustrates them with examples. These examples and explanations will be repeated consistently to ensure that students can remember and state the correct "understanding" of the concept. Before a test or quiz there is a review to check to see if students remember the information and determine where they need to study more. Then the students are tested to see if they remember what they have learned and then move on to the next chapter.

In reality... Let's talk about what needs to transpire in our educational world and classrooms. When you think back to teachers that you felt you learned the most from, what did they have in common? Was it that they were consistent in explaining concepts in the same way again and again and used repetition to ensure your memorization of the concept? Although this is technically not an incorrect way to teach some concepts, it's simply not enough for all students or all types of learning. We have learned over the years that our students have multiple intelligences and some students' intelligences are more dominant than others. These intelligences range from having inclinations towards music, visual displays, verbal-linguistic, logical-mathematical, bodily-kinesthetic, interpersonal, and finally intrapersonal skills. Although some students may be stronger in more than one intelligence, most will find that they struggle to be great at many or all of them. The natural downfall of some teachers is that they also have a dominant intelligence with which they feel most comfortable teaching. It takes a truly responsive teacher to recognize not only what her dominant intelligence is, but to also recognize what her students' intelligences are and to respond to them appropriately to ensure student learning.

Try to finish the following phrases. "Choosy mothers choose _____," or, "Melt in your mouth, not in your_____," or, "Plop! Plop! Fizz! Fizz! Oh what a _____ _____ ___." Although these are merely examples of catchy commercial quotes that have stuck with us all, have you ever wondered why they have stayed with you over the years? My theory is that it's not just the repetition, but there has to be something deeper about the creativity that was utilized in the design of the quote. Notice that the first two don't even rhyme. You may have assumed that they were easy to place into your permanent memory base because you have heard them repeated so many times. In reality, you must have remembered them for some other reason. They were creative and reached you in multiple ways.

So let's look more closely at these catchy commercial tunes. Some of you might remember them because you have a dominant music intelligence and you remember the tune. Others might remember them because they are very visual and can recall what the commercial actually looked like while you were watching it. Others, still, might recall the end of the phrases because they are very verbal and heard it said so many times that it was then committed to memory. My theory on why these commercials are so effective is because they are hitting multiple intelligences to ensure they are reaching their entire audience. Truly responsive and creative teachers also do this every day.

In my attempts to define what a creative teacher is, I have asked my current 8th grade students. They were given a simple Google form that asked them to name the best, creative teacher they ever had and then express what made that teacher so effective and creative. They were also asked to give advice to pre-service teachers that were getting ready to enter the field. Every single response from students involved being fun or optimistic. Table 8.1 summarizes the phrases that came up consistently.

Do you see the trend on the left column? All of them involve the word "fun" in some capacity. When I first saw this, I was surprised because I did not personally associate being creative with being fun. But, leave it to students to define creativity so simply. Being creative should be fun for students. I could probably end this chapter here because I'm not sure anything else I say could

TABLE 8.1   *Student advice to pre-service teachers.*

Try fun things to do	Try different things
Fun games	Always smile
Fun person	Stay positive
Fun personality	Made us laugh
Fun setting	Get the students to enjoy what they are doing
Fun activities	Upbeat
Fun person	Loving your job
Make it fun	Enthusiastic demeanor
Fun and modern	
Have fun learning	

be as true and explicit as telling teachers to make being in their classrooms and learning an enjoyable experience for students. If they are having fun while learning, they're going to be more attentive and ultimately learn more from you. Although the students' definitions suffice for the meaning of a creative teacher, I would like to include some of my own examples from over the years to hopefully help you see what this creative "fun" may look like.

When I was in 8th grade, my teacher, Mrs. Avant, required us to learn a "helping verb" song. This song went to the tune of Jingle Bells and melodically recited "am, is, are, was, were, be, being, been, has had, have, can, could, should, would, might, may, must, will, shall, do, does, did- HEY!" This song had some hand movements, a catchy melody, and was recited by every student in the 8th grade. It was frankly... fun. The only fault I could place on Mrs. Avant was the requirement that all students had to individually perform the song in front of the class. While I watched students perspire and fret over their upcoming performance, I noticed that all the students did indeed easily learn the song. Although I learned this song back in 1997, I still not only know the song, but I also teach it to my students every year. I would like to note, however, that I do not require my students to perform it individually in front of the class. In thinking back on why this was an effective method of teaching helping verbs, I believe it's because it was a creative way to involve more than one multiple intelligence.

Another example of a creative approach to teaching is the way that I teach vocabulary. Traditional ways of teaching vocabulary through memorizing lists, written definitions and quizzes may or may not lead to a student's understanding and use of the words in the future. I feel it is imperative to teach vocabulary in context rather than in isolation. Every day my students learn a new word that is incorporated into a sentence, that put together, makes an entire story for the school year. I include my students' names in the story and make it completely fictional, fun, and frankly, ridiculous for our entertainment. It's a creative, fun way for the students to get involved with grammar and vocabulary. When they encounter the vocabulary word for the day, they will first attempt to define it using the context of the sentence. After several guesses and interpretations of the word, we will then look it up online so we can use the pronunciation tool. Together the students and I will determine what definition we would like to use to define the word and an appropriate motion to represent the word. Because we add a new word every day, we will then practice the words from the day before. The students will stand up, face our word wall with all of the vocabulary, and as I say the vocabulary word, they will then recite the definition and correlating motion. Since there are 180 days of school, by the end of the year, the students have acquired approximately 180 vocabulary words that they have then been using in their daily language and writing. As the year progresses these words become increasingly present in students' comments and legitimately contextualize as part of our classroom talk. The words that I decided to use in my story have come from multiple sources. Some have been inspired as I read adolescent literature and note words that the students may not know but are used frequently. Others come from the SAT word list as I realize that milestone isn't as far from their current reality as they think it is.

When I first started using this method of vocabulary teaching, I was unsure of its long-term impact on my students' lives. It wasn't until I was coaching track for the high school and was talking to one of my former students that I realized most of the vocabulary words and their meanings had been retained. Guillermo, who I taught in 5th grade, was a senior at the high school. While we were driving on the loud bus to one of our meets, he yelled out, "Mrs. Hall, quiz me on my words!" It took some more prodding and explanation from him for me to understand he meant the vocabulary that we had practiced seven years prior. Although my word list evolves every year, I knew there were some words that were always included. I yelled "commenced," and half the bus yelled, "started" and put both hands in front of them where they moved them simultaneously forward to symbolize the start of something. There are moments like this when you realize that you may have actually made a difference to a few students. In reflection on why this method of vocabulary acquisition was effective, I believe it goes back to including multiple ways for students to learn. Of course there was repetition (just like seeing the same commercials multiple times), but the students also saw the word, heard the word, had a kinesthetic motion for the word, and learned it within the context of a sentence that they could go back and refer to for clarification. It was actually after my experience with Guillermo that I commenced (see how I used that word there for you?!!?) using more SAT words in my list. I had the epiphany that if they were going to retain these word lists in their heads, I should ensure that it would help them beyond their everyday reading and writing. I wanted this knowledge of words that they were learning from me in middle school (and sometimes sooner) to be able to impact their success later on.

It should also be noted that as the years have progressed, the word list and correlating definitions have also evolved. There are some years when we looked up a definition, and as I naturally wanted to use the same definition that I used previously, the students had questions or comments that led us to a different wording of the meaning that made sense to them. They learned to analyze how the meanings of words within current contexts have been altered and had different associations with the word (such as the word "epic" becoming trendy and increasingly used incorrectly in my students' conversations), or they found a more meaningful and effective way of defining it (for them) than students I had before. I feel it is important to listen to the students, respond to their questions and comments, and let them help me create learning with them. Every class is different and should be treated as a unique group with its own set of needs, and a disposition towards being creative helps this to be an exciting challenge instead of a daunting task.

Although this one way of teaching vocabulary is an example of being a creative teacher, a truly creative, responsive teacher is not going to emerge from changing the way you teach grammar. I believe that the key is in your relationship with the students. By getting to know your students, you have the ability to reach them on a much deeper level. I find that humor is a staple in my classroom. Because I know my students well, I can include comments about something funny that happened in our room/on the field/at lunch/in the hall within my teaching. I'll use parts of an experience they've told me about in our daily grammar or when I'm modeling a writing technique. I'll even personalize examples from our literature by connecting them with something one of the students has gone through. These little examples from the students' lives gets them more involved in learning and genuinely makes the classroom a fun place to be. In addition, not only do I often know experiences that have happened to them, but I take time to share my own personal experiences.

My oldest son, Brody, has always been a handful, which naturally leads to the best stories to share with my students. Often my classroom will be engaged in an activity when I'll be reminded of yet another "Brody story" (that's what my students inevitably call this time). Sometimes I'll chuckle and tell them, "okay, if I tell you one more Brody story, you promise to work extra hard to make up for the time?" They always brighten up and beg to hear about another shenanigan from my rambunctious little guy. I remember seeing a former student of mine and her asking, "Remember the time you told us about Brody shoving Q-tips in both ears and jumping on the bed? That was the best!"

At first, I always thought I was losing valuable teaching time giving in and telling them stories. Later I realized taking the time to interact with my students through stories (that at least were usually related to our activity!) helped me build a relationship with them. It's through that relationship that I am then able to pass on knowledge. The students need to see you have fun; they need to see you as a real person/mom/wife/struggling afternoon teacher and mentor that cares about them. That means laughing every day, doing the Cupid Shuffle at the middle school dance, asking the kids if their dog had puppies yet, and incorporating their (and your) unique personalities into the classroom.

So if you're reading this chapter on how to be a responsively disposed, creative instructional leader and you're still searching for either the "right" way, or even affirmation that what you're doing is working, remember what Alan Alda once said. "The creative is the place where no one else has ever been. You have to leave the city of your comfort and go into the wilderness of your intuition. What you'll discover will be wonderful. What you'll discover is yourself." So I suggest that you start by listening to your students, and respond to what they have to say. This will help you to find and create more pathways to reach each diverse learner and continue the journey to reaching your students. Or simply put... have fun!

CHAPTER 9

Management: The Disposition to Empower
by Kim Tufts

> Education is not the filling of a pail, but the lighting of a fire.
> WILLIAM BUTLER YEATS

Technically speaking... A good teacher makes sure that students know who is "the boss" in a classroom. Students must earn respect from the teacher by first showing respect to the teacher. In order to maintain a safe and orderly classroom, a good teacher will not allow disruptive and inappropriate behavior and rules will be clearly posted and restated as often as necessary to make sure that students follow them. A zero-tolerance policy will quickly establish a proper power structure and eliminate undesirable behaviors. Technically speaking, all students should be treated the same in the interest of being fair. There needs to be very clear boundaries so that students know that their teacher is not their friend. A good teacher will not share personal information, stories, or perspectives so that the classroom is free of bias and stays focused on the task at hand. Technically speaking, the classroom of a good teacher is often quiet, clean, and well organized. It should display only the best of all student work so that students know what good work looks like. The classroom of a good teacher will be bright and cheerful, organization bins will be tidy and color-coordinated, and students will have designated work areas.

Technically speaking, these teachers and classrooms exist and some of them are also truly warm and inviting places to learn. But teaching transcends technicalities. Teaching is an art. It is grounded in its technical foundations, yet fluidly interacts with the culture and people it is serving in such a way as to create and adapt to the learning environment responsively.

In reality... Teaching is an art that is individual, even personal, and yet nuanced by the people within it. In the last 25 years, I have never had a group of students before me that was exactly like another group. As I brought my self, my pedagogy, and my curriculum to each new group, I found that the end result each time was a new classroom dynamic and a changed self. It is that very aspect of teaching that draws me and makes each year different and special to me. I miss each class as they move on, yet I am excited to encounter the next class!

In the first few years of teaching, I was advised to start the school year with as much strictness and toughness as possible. Veterans told me that it was easier to relax established discipline than it was to tighten up as behaviors required. It made sense. And, it does work. Over the years, however, my personality came to bear on that practice and I found that I was so energized by meeting my new classes on those first days of school that I was friendly and even...bouncy. What I found was that students responded to my positive energy with their own positive energy! When disruptive behaviors were exhibited and I made my own natural responses – disappointment, lowered energy, brevity of speech – they didn't like the change in my behavior and our classroom atmosphere. They adjusted their behaviors to maintain the environment that they preferred! I began to acknowledge the role that bringing my "self" to the classroom played in the mutual satisfaction we felt in our established classroom culture.

From the time I was a little girl, my family noticed that I had a nurturing personality. In the 1960's, that was referred to as a natural "mommy." I loved being a big sister, feeding little animals, growing flowers, and helping in any way that I was encouraged. As I grew older, the "mommy" label was adjusted to "teacher." I was constantly creating classrooms of my neighborhood playmates and "teaching" them. This consisted of chalkboard lessons on spelling and math, followed by tests. Looking back now, I am chagrined. I am saddened by my early impressions of teaching – skill drills and testing! I truly can't imagine how I kept friends, or even why kids would have kept coming back to my "school." My reflections on these experiences encouraged me to embrace my need to nurture and to desire an element of fun in my professional classroom.

In reality, I do have expectations and structure in my classroom. I am absolutely insistent on respect – of each other and our environment. I have found that respect covers a multitude of character traits that I find desirable in my classroom. It covers traits like integrity, kindness, consideration, collegiality, timeliness, cleanliness, and frugality. I encourage the development of responsibility and self-control. I model those tenets that I am encouraging, but I also acknowledge my own failures as they arise – coupled with my plan for future improvement based on that learning experience. For instance, our district is a one-to-one computer district. Students and their families must go through training on computer care before they can take their computer home. Some of the basic guidelines are to keep food and drink away from their computer and to keep the computer on a flat surface. Teachers, however, were not put through the same "training" and so I continued the habits I had developed over the years with my own laptops. One afternoon, I went home and made a mug of tea before I sat down in my recliner with my computer. Even now, several years later, I cringe at the inevitability of this scenario. I hadn't been working very long when I apparently fell asleep, causing the mug to tip and fill my lap with moderately hot water. I awoke immediately, of course, and was overcome with panic about my computer. However, after examination, I felt that the tea must have just emptied on me, with a little in my computer cover. I put the tea away and resumed activity. After dinner, when I returned to my computer, it was a different story. The computer was giving me a coded error message that seemed to require a technician. I took it in to school, filed a help ticket, and they retrieved my computer. The bottom line was that I had gotten tea into the hard drive and I was going to have to pay for the repair… to the tune of several hundred dollars…on a computer that I didn't actually own. I shared the story with my students as a cautionary tale. What ensued were a series of very relevant classroom discussions centered on honesty and responsibility. You can imagine their advice to me as to what I could have done differently to avoid the fees! The final lesson I shared was that I purchased non-spill containers to use when working with my computer. I can still drink, but no longer have the danger of getting liquid in my keyboard. I have found that students are so responsive to teachers who are learning *with* them!

In reality, I find that my students and I have a lot in common. It really doesn't matter that the age difference is increasing between us. We still both want others to know what's going on in our lives and to care about the things that are important to us. We both want to feel like others approve of us. Understanding that means recognizing that the term "zero-tolerance" has to be modified with care and consideration for each individual and situation. It also has to include the balance of consistency and firmness that underlies responsive discipline. Ultimately, it is not really zero tolerance.

I spent several years working in a public charter school that served students in a residential treatment center. These children, Kindergarten through twelfth grade, had been removed from abusive environments and were receiving counseling and training on how to cope with their pasts and stop the cycle from continuing. It was our mode to promote zero tolerance as a way of providing a safe environment. In my self-contained, teen male, reduced-class-size environment, we dealt with emotional and behavioral crises every hour of our classroom time. The concept of zero tolerance was not something I could enforce on my own, and I quickly recognized the danger of creating power struggles. Imagine an average height female commanding an emotionally charged, behaviorally reckless, teen male to stop an undesirable behavior – because she said so. That is not a battle that will be won by that female. In fact, that is the formula that basically guarantees escalation of undesirable behavior. What I found that worked better was to build a classroom environment that the students appreciated, and then encourage everyone to maintain that status quo. For my group of guys, that included project-based and inquiry-based instruction where their interests were not only valued, but supported. It meant a classroom where they could regularly share what they had discovered or created. It meant that self-control was rewarded with increased opportunities to explore outside of the classroom – a true exchange of mutual respect that kept strengthening.

From my years in that environment, I also learned which behaviors needed to be addressed and which needed to be overlooked. After working with children who exhibited extremes in out-of-control behavior, like turning over bookshelves and unleashing streams of directed ugly language, more commonplace "bad behaviors" in the regular public school were not threatening. What I found was that foundational expectation of respect covered the ever-changing classroom landscape and required that we all – teacher and students alike – consider what made our classroom feel safe and inviting. I hold the line at following our school and county policies because respecting authority and law will most likely lead my students to longer, freer, and more productive lives. I hold classroom discussions about how to be part of the change process when there is authority or law that we believe needs alteration. This provides a sense of power and control for students who are ripe for that knowledge developmentally. Simultaneously, I loosen up some of the classroom restrictions they have felt in previous years in response to extended demonstration of self-control. In my classroom, it is possible to have flexible seating choice that could include lying on the floor, sitting in a corner, putting feet on their desk, or standing. It is possible to be able to sit wherever you want from day to day, without teacher-assigned seating. It is possible to propose an alternative way to complete an assignment or even an alternative text to use for the assignment. For classes that are able to achieve the classroom objectives in a timely manner, it is even possible to create a topic for class study or design a mini-unit. The bottom line is that the more students recognize their perspectives, interests, and ideas are valued, the less discipline and management that has to take place.

In reality, when the discipline and management balance is in place, the relational balance is much easier to shape. My students know that I am in charge of our classroom, both instructionally and physically. But they also know that I am there to serve them, guide them, learn with them, and grow with them. That makes us a team, working together for common goals. They know their voice is valued, collectively and individually, and they tell me that they can see me working to balance all of their input with what they are there to learn. I think that transparency is an important aspect in what makes my classroom work, too. There are times when I am so discouraged or even frustrated and I lay out my concerns to them. Sometimes it is a management challenge that is not getting worked out and sometimes it is an objective that we are not accomplishing. They always give me feedback. It's not always realistic, but they get to think aloud with me as we process ideas. Occasionally, students bring requests for change of assignment, due date, or even seating.

As often as feasible, I give them permission to problem-solve that issue with me. In the same way, our classroom is able to tackle hard topics. All honest and earnest voices and perspectives are valued and given time. Really. On rare occasions, I have had to point out that we didn't seem ready to handle discussing a certain issue because the listening aspect had fallen away. But students are generally disappointed in these outcomes and work to avoid it in the future. I have found that students want their important issues to be heard and I know that we'll learn more of our speaking/listening objectives in this relevant discussion than in top-down initiatives. In this environment, I have learned that my classes appreciate my anecdotes – short or long, relevant or off-topic! Through these stories I become a much more relatable person, and I find students telling me important stories about their lives because they know from my own stories that I'll understand. This is probably the area that I struggle the most as a teacher, though. I love to tell stories! One of the structures I have put in place to curb my own potential for off-task behavior, is actually my students as story monitors. As we get to know each other, and I begin to tell stories, I instruct them to remember that we need to achieve our classroom objectives each day to most successfully complete our year. I share the perspective that they need to own their success and not let anything get in their way – including their story-telling teacher! I promise that my role will be to make sure they complete our assignments, so that if they let me use up too much class time in off-task behavior they will still have to complete their assignment, but now it will need to be independent. We only have to live that promise out one time, and the students recognize the control they have and actually make choices! Occasionally they tell me that they want me to keep telling a story, that they can handle completing the work, and then sometimes they tell me they would like to hear it...some other time! It's awesome! I find that being open to my students' (and their parents') feedback is equally valuable to my growth as an individual and practitioner as my own reflections. Here is some of the feedback I've received that supports how I feel about relationships in the classroom:

> I just want to say thank you so much. I have never had a teacher that cares as much as you do about your students. You are not just a teacher in my opinion. I personally see you as a role model and an inspiration. Thank you for caring so much about us and helping me learn not only in English but in all kinds of life skills. (8th grade student)
>
> ___ was home today with a flu-like virus. Waiting to see if she feels well enough to go to school tomorrow. She has been reading, *Little Men* by Louisa May Alcott. I just went to tuck her in and she said, "Mrs. Tufts

reminds me of Jo. She has the respect of the whole class. She lets us have fun but knows how to keep order." What a great compliment for an amazing teacher. ___ has learned so much in your class – not just content but about herself as a reader, writer, thinker and learner. She adores you! We are so thankful for you. Keep up the good work! (8th grade parent)

In reality, the space in which we work, the classroom, is there for the students. I spend a lot of time in that room, so I want it to be a comfortable place that is attractive to me. But I am also a compulsively obsessive person who needs to have a place for everything and everything in its place at the end of the day. The world that makes sense to me is one that is organized and coordinated. My husband tells me that it is my inner elementary school teacher and my inner librarian battling it out in the confines of my classroom. I tell my students that my organization and structure allows their time in the classroom to be more productive. I am the manager of the space and the materials on behalf of the school and for the benefit of present and future students. Ultimately, the room belongs to all of us. It is *our* classroom. I have set up the room to be as inviting to them as it is comfortable to me. I wrote a grant and received monies for three commercial grade carpets and some patio furniture. The carpets are each different dynamic patterns using our school colors. There are curtains at the window for a softer, less institutional feel, and the patio furniture is sturdy with some padding. There are bookshelves with books for the students to use in class and to check out to take home. There is a tower that my husband built that houses project materials and paper. A separate grant provided a rolling kitchen cart that houses everything needed for classroom food preparation in relation to our units. On a side note, I need to explain that I use it to connect with cultures and times in our texts, but also for celebrations and with advisory for teaching life skills. Hey, I understand it might not be for every teacher, but I have found that food is unifying, memorable, and appeals to a multitude of senses! Also appealing to the senses in my classroom, is a plug-in with cloves and cinnamon. Those scents are good for energizing and remembering but have the extra benefit of connecting to happy memories like baked goods and holidays. Most desks are at the center of it all and able to be flexibly arranged for a variety of contexts. A few larger desks are ganged together to form a meeting table at the side of the room for small groups and conferences. The goal is a comfortable learning environment. My desk sits in the back corner in a nook I designed for my tasks. I ask students to respect that area as my personal space and as the appropriately confidential space for their work. Therefore, it is the only area in the classroom that is not open to them, unless they are coming to talk with me.

Of course the ultimate room decorations are the students' work. I have four small square bulletin boards in our room. One of them always highlights our classroom expectations. Sometimes I use one or two to post unit materials. However, I have found that it really helps validate their work and build a sense of pride when we work together to create displays of their work. We have space in the hall we can use, too. It shocks me how often an eighth grader will get teary-eyed because they don't remember ever having their work displayed before. I have even had students tell me that their work probably shouldn't go out for everyone to see because it isn't good enough! It seems to me that there are two important responses for that. The first is to ask *why* they don't think it's good enough, and therefore what they can do differently next time (or this time, if they want to redo). The second is to point out that everyone's work is important. We can learn so much from the work and perspectives of others.

And, in reality, that is the gift we are given from our students each and every year. Their energy, perspectives, and fresh hope for their futures are contagious. Their struggles and victories throughout their time with us are inspirational. In reality, I have found that they inform and empower my work as a teacher and my life outside of school.

CHAPTER 10

Management: The Disposition to Connect
by Brooke Huffman

People will forget what you said, people will forget what you did, but
people will never forget how you made them feel.
    MAYA ANGELOU

Technically speaking... Students should be sitting calmly at their desks, paying
rapt attention to the teacher who stands at the board (a safe distance away
both physically and mentally) imparting her knowledge while the students
take notes. These students are allowed to ask or answer questions when the
teacher calls on them. The teacher would have taught this lesson many times
in previous years the same way each year for each class because it meets the
standards. There would be no need to change the lesson because at least eighty
percent of the students were on grade level last year and the rest of the twenty
percent are projected to be below because they have an IEP or some other
problem. The dialogue in this classroom would only be centered on this lesson
and any student who was not on task would be sent to the office for immediate
punishment.

Some people have this picture in their head of the perfect classroom.
Technically speaking, this is what a good teacher should do. But, this is simply
not reality. In this case, reality is a lot more promising. A real classroom looks
and operates in a much different way. Classroom management was the one
topic I wanted to learn the most about as a teacher candidate. The idea that
I would be the only one in front of and responsible for a class of hormonal,
puberty-ridden thirteen year olds was terrifying in the least!

In reality... You will see, as teachers we have this awesome task. It is a task
that we embrace. How many times have we said the only reason we teach is
because of the students? This isn't just a colloquialism. This is real and true.
We are blessed to teach students who are curious, searching, optimistic and
hopeful, yet self-conscious, needing acceptance, figuring out life and personal
beliefs–all while coping with physical and emotional changes from minute to
minute. All students are valuable and each one has unique qualities that make
him/her capable of learning and "being the best me" that they can be.
Students deserve to have an adult advocate in their lives who has high
expectations; gives consistent encouragement; promotes academic, social,
and emotional learning; treats them with mutual respect; and truly invests in

their academic and personal lives. Students need to feel loved, encouraged, celebrated, and safe because the teacher strives to understand what their personal interests are, what struggles they are facing, what academic needs they have, what they want for their future, and what moral/ethical ideas they are developing. A teacher must go the extra mile that it takes to earn the trust of the students by talking to them, communicating with their parents and other important people in their lives, and giving them opportunities to discuss relevant topics that are affecting them. Teachers must encourage students to recognize and tap into their potential, look to find the good and unique qualities in all of their students, and create lessons tailored to encouraging students to learn about themselves, their peers, and the world around them.

We teachers are entrusted to empower students, our future leaders, our precious treasures. Empowering is a word that brings great responsibility. Empowering implies creating a sense of intrinsic motivation. Empowering is making people stronger and more confident especially in controlling their lives. It is a word that defines a teacher and our life's work. It is what we hope to impart to each one of our students. How do we go about empowering someone? Why should a student listen to you and the wisdom you espouse? Why do you even care if a person is happy or does well in life? Why would a student care what an old lady has to say? The answer is simple– because we care. Students must know that a teacher cares. Students must know and feel connected to their teacher with a relationship built on trust, caring, encouragement, sincerity, and a bond that is unbroken no matter the circumstance. This connection is what we must create and foster because it is precious. Without this connection, there can be no empowerment, no learning, no future. When a student feels safe and can trust, then there is true, authentic classroom management based on respect, respect for each other, other students, and more importantly for oneself.

This connectivity is the basis of a teacher's ability to maintain control or management within the classroom. Classroom management is such a broad topic, but one that encompasses so many aspects of how teachers and students interact with each other. Being able to ensure that learning happens everyday depends on preventative measures. The groundwork for my style of classroom management is laid from the very first day that I meet a student. I work hard to make sure that my students know that I care. I care about each one of them. At my school, we set aside a day at the end of the school year we call "Move Up Day." On this day, the students visit the classrooms of their teachers for the next school year. This is my first opportunity to assure the students that the next year of his/her life is going to be one that he/she will never forget. We, myself and the other teachers, promise the students that we will have a good year where we work hard and enjoy the learning that comes with it. On this day, I enjoy seeing the new crop of students' faces and looking to recognize the brothers and sisters of students that I have already taught. You see, this connection is important to a student because they like to know that you have a sense of who they are, what they need, and where they come from. This is the beginning of a relationship that will be lasting. This is the beginning of a relationship that consists of students coming back to see me, emailing me, telling their professors about creative assignments they did in my class, and former parents contacting me to keep me updated on them. The year that we spend together promotes a lasting relationship.

On the very first day of school, I give my students homework. Can you believe that? Homework to read a letter that I write to each one of them. In my letter, I tell each student about myself- where I grew up, about my family, what I love to do in my free time, etc... I ask the students to write me back. This is such a simple task, but one that gives me my first little window into their lives and their needs- academically and emotionally speaking. But it also serves another purpose. I become a real person to the student. A real person who has a life, interests, family. I become a person that is willing to share about myself in the hopes that it will be reciprocated. In reading their letters, I learn valuable information about them- what the students believe are their strengths and what they need to work on. It's incredible how students warm up to you when they have a common ground or understanding of their teacher.

Before school even starts, I have already spoken to our school social worker, the students' resource teacher, and any other teacher that knows these students. I ask the teacher before me how to pronounce and spell each student's name. Something this simple tells the students that you care- you care enough to know their name. I like to be prepared, so that I can treat my students as individuals. I study data about the students like grade level assessments, progress monitoring, Individual Education Plans, attendance reports, etc... I send out surveys to parents and ask them to tell me about their child's strengths, weaknesses, and good things I need to know. I survey the students and ask them about their thoughts on reading success, struggles, and what they like to read. On that first day, I make it a point to learn each of my new students' names. This can be a daunting task when you teach 90 or more students. But again, knowing something as simple as a name helps create a sense of caring.

I work to create a sense of community in the classroom that helps the students to feel as if they have entered into a family environment in which we all care for each other and ourselves. From the beginning, I am careful to set simple guidelines that we are all expected to follow: respect yourself, respect others, and respect others' property and the environment. Guidelines must be general, obvious, and easy to follow. And they must be followed consistently. Students want structure. They want an adult in their lives that provide guidelines and rules that must be followed. Sometimes, the teacher is the only one that can fulfill that need. Teachers must be fair. In the first week of school, we read each of the school rules and talk about them. For example, I have students read through our school norms. They love to talk about how their grade level does at following the rules and deciding what to work on as a grade level. The group I am teaching this year is a known group of talkers that got into trouble many times last year for loud behavior in the hallway. So, we talked about it. Talked... Not fussed at, but talked. I explained that after having been at a workshop and sitting still for several hours, I understood how hard it would be to not be allowed to talk during a break. The students saw the connection to their situation. A student then pointed out how it can be distracting when students are loud in the hallway. So, together we decided that they could whisper in the hallway. And guess what? It didn't work perfectly the first few times. Here's where respect comes into play. The natural tendency is to fuss at the students, but I have found greater success when I ask them to remember what they decided about whispering. Kids respond to the ability to make changes based on their own ideas.

If a student chooses not to follow the guidelines, then I am quick to pull him/her aside and find out exactly what the motivation is behind the action. Students need an adult to follow through and hold him/her accountable for their actions and behavior. Teachers always have to remember that we are the adults. The students will test us to see if we will cut and walk away from him/her. We must not take misbehavior personally. We have to draw the line between adult and child and lead the child back to the right path. Again, be fair, be consistent, but care.

It is important for a teacher to make sure that the procedures of the classroom are clear. A teacher needs to plan ahead and have a clear idea of how things should run in the classroom. And then they need to teach the students how to do them. Simple things like knowing when and how a student is allowed to sharpen a pencil, to get water from the fountain at the back of the room, or even how to work with a group will help to make the day run smoothly and be conducive to learning. Preparing students ahead of time will greatly reduce the instances of misbehavior or students not being on task. When we know our expectations, then we rise to them.

Any time a teacher can include input from students on instructional strategies, assessments, and curriculum then buy in happens and students will be successful. When Drake said, "Mrs. Huffman, you should use Flocabulary.

It really helps me remember vocabulary words," I got trained, starting using it, and realized that Drake was right! Chances are that if it helps him, then other students in the class will benefit too. Being responsive to individual differences in developmental needs helps to build an inclusive community within the classroom. Emphasizing progress and regularly encouraging students must follow. Students need to be recognized in different ways, be it a pat on the back, words of encouragement, a call home to a parent, a formal award, the compliment you give a student with a new haircut or new glasses... whatever it takes to make sure that a student knows that you noticed. Because when you care, then they care. They care and want to succeed.

We, as teachers, have been entrusted to nurture and shape our future. We have been given the opportunity to make a difference. Our life's work is meaningful and important. Without a teacher, what would the world be? Without that teacher that takes you and brings you ten steps forward, where would you be? We, as teachers, do have an awesome responsibility and with great responsibility comes great expectations. Teachers know "it"!

We can all do it. We can all tell exactly who our favorite teachers were and we can distinctly tell you why. That's how important and lasting a teacher's impact can be. We can put ourselves back in that classroom and see the teacher or even tell a special story about a special teacher who changed your life, a teacher who saw your potential and encouraged you to follow it, a teacher who made learning fun, made the learning just seem like something fun you are supposed to do. As a teacher, I strive to be like them. What better way to honor a teacher than to try to follow in his or her footsteps. We, as teachers, want to ensure that we are reaching our students. How better to do this, than to ask them what they think makes a good teacher? Students can give us helpful pieces of advice of what they need.

So, I asked them (my seventh graders) "What do you think makes a good teacher?" It's interesting because all of the answers were mainly the same. No, not the silly things—like good teachers take us outside, don't give a lot of homework, and let us take a nap. These are not the answers I got. The overall theme of each of the answers is for teachers to know and care about their students. Sounds familiar, huh? Students know when they are in a safe place and are cared for. Students crave the basic human need of care. One student said simply, a good teacher has respect for his/her students and for himself/herself. Another student said, a good teacher teaches their class to respect and like them and then the class won't act up. He goes on to say, but most of all, a good teacher loves their class, as if they were his/her own children. This is a powerful statement- the love of a parent being applied to the love of a teacher. The definition of love begets compassion, care, concern, friendliness, kindness, sympathy, unselfishness, and benevolence. Students want to know that a teacher won't yell at the students, won't call them names, won't call on them and embarrass them in front of the whole class when they don't know the right answer, and won't punish the whole class because one person is causing a problem. Students want a teacher who is strict, but strict in the way that shows caring. If a teacher has a high standard for her students and won't accept anything less, students will rise to that challenge. They need it. One student said her favorite teacher was relatable. They all liked her and she liked them. Simple.

Another theme that is evident in the students' responses is for teachers to solve conflicts and problems privately. Students want to know that a teacher will work to make lessons that reach all levels of comprehension. If a student doesn't understand, then the teacher will go back and help that one student individually. One girl writes, if a student needs help, the teacher should meet with the student before or after school to make sure they understand. Students really do want to learn and be successful. They depend on the adults in their lives to make that happen. Students want teachers to deal with conflicts as they arise, to not wait until it's too late. They want teachers to step in and hear both sides of the story and to not assume anything. Another student writes, a good teacher solves problems without making them public. It is important for a teacher to be there for both people and to help them through the conflict and come out on the other side better than before. A good trait for a teacher to have is a passion for their students.

When it comes to style, students want a teacher who makes learning fun. They need a teacher who creates lessons that meet individual learning styles. They want a teacher who has a sense of humor, but one that always remembers to teach so that each student understands. They want teachers to be certain that all students understand the lesson before moving on. This is mentioned over and over. They want us to keep them thinking and learning constantly- be it with a presentation or a project. They also ask that we have a fun, energetic attitude every day because it is contagious. Enjoyment in learning becomes contagious.

One student explains what makes a good teacher perfectly. She writes, not everyone is fit for being a good teacher. It takes a special type of person that has a kind heart, but can also teach valuable life lessons. It takes a teacher that possesses "it."

I was one of the lucky ones. I truly had one of the best mentors a new teacher could have. Mrs. Cooper, my friend, my teacher-hero taught me the true gift of being a teacher. She took this scared first year teacher and showed me, modeled for me, how a teacher/student relationship should look and how it should work. I have read so many young adult novels, that I am able to help match books to students' interests so hopefully I can foster their love of reading. I listen when a student needs me to, I watch their interactions, and I simply try to be aware. Bottom line, I work to make sure my students know that I truly am trying to understand their needs and strengths. I am connected to them.

CHAPTER 11

Professionalism: The Disposition towards Change
by Kellie Johnson

> Those who cannot change their minds cannot change anything.
> GEORGE BERNARD SHAW

Technically speaking... A professional teacher is concerned with following mandates and directives. It is the teacher's job to make sure that standards, procedures, and guidelines are followed and that expectations for her performance are met. Above all, a professional teacher exhibits self-control when in staff meetings or while serving on committees. Many feel that this is exhibited by not calling too much attention to oneself. Speaking out, expressing opinions, and asking too many questions is disruptive to school meetings and the school's achievement goals. Questioning the principal or other administrators is disrespectful and may cost you your job. Professionalism means being respectful and kind to reach consensus. The teacher who keeps things running smoothly in the school by getting along with others will get the rewards she deserves.

The word "Professional" brings to mind images of business suits, briefcases, meeting rooms, and stoic adults in a pristine office setting, but what does the word "teacher" bring to mind? When conjuring up images of "teacher" each of us sees real people who touched our lives in a personal way. Some will see a woman sitting cross-legged on the floor reading Dr. Seuss, some will see a grey-haired man in safety goggles lighting a Bunsen burner, and others will hear the voice that still rings in their subconscious decades later saying, "Give me your best, not your least!"

In reality... Teachers do not deal with products, numbers, and quotas, but rather they deal with humans – the most difficult "product" to manage. A truly professional teacher realizes that he or she is accountable for the education of his or her students, and sometimes being the best teacher is not in line with being the best "employee." So how does professionalism manifest itself in educational dispositions? Let's break down this concept into categories.

The concept of a compliance-focused disposition is clear from the name. Those who lean toward this attitude are the followers of the world. They are mostly concerned with following the given mandates and directives. They like structure, patterns, and a strong leader figure. These teachers do not want to disrupt the status quo, do not want to draw attention to themselves or to their

© KONINKLIJKE BRILL NV, LEIDEN, 2018 | DOI 10.1163/9789004364486_011

school. They are comfortable in a cookie-cutter world – looking, acting, and being like the model educator. These are the "Stepford Wives" in education; they look good, say the right things, please their leaders, but do not dare think for themselves or fight for their students. When we picture an educator in our mind, this teacher is like a grey ghost; we remember having a math teacher in 7th grade, but we don't even remember if that person was a man or woman.

In contrast, the Change-driven educator seeks to make a positive difference in the educational world. Change-driven educators understand the need for a healthy balance of professionalism as both rule following, and rule challenging. A change-driven educator is concerned with the improvement of education as a whole. These educators focus on research-based action and continually seek the most relevant and reliable research to develop ideas and plans for the world of education. In fact, the change-driven educator is often the one working, planning and creating the newest research results for the educational field. The change driven educator continually seeks professional growth for him/herself and encourages others to grow and improve. While not blindly seeking out new ways to break the rules and go against the status quo, a change-driven educator is not afraid to question those in power and push for answers, evidence, and positive change. These teachers are the movers, shakers, and destiny makers of the educational world. This description sounds like a change-driven educator will have her own theme music and be lauded as a great leader in her school. Wouldn't that be great?

Recently I worked with two other educators on a three man academic team in our middle school. We all taught the same group of students and worked together to plan instruction and meet student needs. In our team meetings, we would discuss ideas for motivating reluctant learners and needs that we saw for all students. These discussions brought out a great idea for motivating students and meeting a pressing need we all saw. Our group of students had several reluctant learners who did not do homework and many of those students did not have a strong support system at home. We also realized that our students did not get much socialization time or daily activity because only half of the students had PE during each semester.

We knew that the gym in our school building was free every day for a one-hour period while the PE teachers had planning. All of these elements seemed to fit together into a great plan for our students. We decided to blend a "recess" time and study hall on Fridays for our students. Students who were missing assignments during the week would go to a classroom and work with one of the teachers to make up work; all of the other students went outside to walk, play and socialize with their friends. The middle school students were so excited to have "recess" at their age. They gave us suggestions about bringing balls for them to play and letting them work on homework outside so that those who needed help could still get fresh air and have the chance to play when they finished their work.

Students began to check with me on Wednesdays and Thursdays to make sure they had all of their work turned in because they wanted to be free to enjoy recess. The number of students needing to make up assignments significantly decreased. I had one student who had been retained the year before and truly showed no motivation to learn suddenly become conscientious about his weekly assignments. An added benefit to recess time was the opportunity we as teachers had to talk with students, see them interact with their friends, get to know them better. All of this seemed like an overwhelming success story to us, but...

We were doing something different. Others in the building noticed that we were outside with our students and we began to get "feedback" from our peers.

"That's not the way we do things around here."

We know. We are trying something new.

"You do this every week? Did you ask administration about this?"

Yes! Our administrator who is a former PE teacher does agree that students benefit from exercise.

"How do you cover your curriculum?"

We use the class time we have wisely.

The first wave of questions died down and we continued our experiment. The students looked forward to Friday. Other students in the building asked their teachers why their team didn't get recess. We were labeled the "fun team," and the next wave of "feedback" came.

"Can you cover my class Friday? I know you're not teaching anyway."

No. I am working with small groups of students or building relationships with my students.

"I just don't think I could spend an hour of my teaching time each week playing."

We are trying to work smarter, not harder. Want to try something new with us?

A few teachers asked us how we worked out our schedule and seemed interested in the plan. One team instituted "Fun Friday" the next year. Others are still watching.

When your peers are watching you as an example of change, it is not easy. There are ways to find support for the innovations you espouse and implement. A good start is to seek and surround yourself with other teachers who are disposed to embrace being a change agent as a major part of their professional identity. Working together, working smart, grounding what you are doing on inquiry or evidence of a specific need helps you to move forward. Connections to research and best practices help to bring interested parents and colleagues into the fold. Understanding your administrator's concerns and needs as well as how best to work with her is fundamental to your progress. Your number one source of support and advocacy is your students. When students see and can articulate the benefits of change to them as learners and people, parents, school board members and others are more likely to keep an open mind and want to learn more about the change. Change-driven educators don't bring about change just for the sake of doing things differently; they see a need and make a plan. Research, data, strategy, and professional responsibility are all key components to a plan of change. A great educator will diligently document, analyze, and revise her strategies to create data and valid research for other educators to build upon. Be the change and then share the plan.

Good educational systems must be "living systems" constantly evolving into a better, more productive system, improving methods, pedagogy, and curriculum. Professional and effective educators must realize that for change to be necessary, it must also be useful, intentional, vetted and thus evidenced in educational research and knowledge base. Articulating the reasons for change to other constituents is vital. Working with parents, colleagues, administrators, and even your students as partners in the change process will improve chances of success. Change should not be implemented for change sake or as the newest educational fad or mandate driven product. The bottom line for professional educators to act as agents of change is to make schools better places for students and students better prepared for happy, powerful and meaningful lives beyond school walls.

CHAPTER 12

Professionalism: The Disposition to Be Inclusive
by Kalie Eppley

> When community, cooperation, and collaborative learning are the prevailing metaphors driving our schools, rather than hierarchy, competition and accountability, then it will follow that issues of voice, participation, ownership and active democracy will be precursors of new leadership patterns, and this is a hard road to travel. It is one of the journeys against the grain.
>
> HELEN GUNTER – LEADING TEACHERS

Technically speaking... An obedient and "good" teacher follows the hierarchy set forth by her state, county, and school. She should follow mandates and directives from the state. She should refrain from questioning or disrupting during faculty meetings. Upper administration and principals are the decision makers and teachers should refrain from asking why and focus on asking how they can implement those decisions. A good teacher should do what is required of her regardless of her opinion and should recognize the authority of the hierarchy above her.

In reality... That fails to include several people in the equation. Education is a partnership. The disposition to be inclusive as a professional educator is demonstrated when a teacher, or preferably school, uses a model of decision-making involving all concerned parties in a child's educational plan, rather than focusing the school on the hierarchy and accountability as driving forces. Ongoing dialogue that is representative of multiple perspectives that reflects an understanding of the role that a whole community plays in a child's education is pervasive. Inclusive professionals are concerned with giving voice to others and listening to what others have to say as they collaboratively engage in decision-making. Education professionals actively seek collaboration, reciprocity, ownership, and leadership from all stakeholders. Being inclusive is an orientation to professionalism that puts the student back at the top of the priority list.

My inclusion story starts long before my first day as a teacher. As a young adolescent student, I walk into school the Monday before the first day of school, hoping to meet my new 6th grade teacher. My mom teaches at my school, so I always go over to her school on teacher workdays to see if I can be of help. One of my teachers for the year is new to the school, so I (or rather my mom) thought that she could probably use some help. I am a true introvert, and the thought of going to introduce myself to this mystery teacher is frightening to say the least. However, hanging out with teachers makes me feel important, so I go. Also, I love being at school. I love the smells and the people. I love coming up with spelling sheets and helping grade my mom's papers. This is my last week before school starts, and I have been waiting all summer to spend it in the empty building doing "teacher things." Nothing compares to this – not the beach trip we went on last month, not my best friend's birthday party at Carowinds, and not hanging out at the pool at noon. I walk down the long middle school wing, relishing the quiet of the hallway and the peace it brings. I knock on her door.

"Hey," I say in a low voice, face red. "I have you this year."

"Hello! Okay now what's your name?"

"Kalie."

She smiled, "I'm Mrs. Huffman."

Fast forward through 11 years, a high school graduation, a bachelor's degree in Middle Grades Education, and a job acceptance at the same school I walked into at the beginning of that unexpectedly pivotal and significant year. As I walk down the hall during this year's teacher workdays, I feel the same peace in my heart. I have all the same excitement as a student ready to play teacher for a day, only now it isn't just for fun. There are high stakes now. I sit in my room, that I had sat in 180 times as a student, for the first time as a teacher. I breathe in the smells of old books, fresh paper, and new wax on the floor. I couldn't wait for the students to roll in on Monday, so that I could begin to share my joy.

As I walk down to the office to check my box for the first time, I see different teachers and staff members that I've known since Kindergarten, and they all seem to say the same things:

"Aren't you so excited to finally have a classroom all your own."

"You finally get to do your own thing; it's not anyone else's class."

"How ready are you? To be on your own."

It takes me a second, because, well, yes I'm ready to have my own classes to teach, and yes I'm very excited. But that's not really how I see it. It isn't *my* classroom. It isn't *my* thing. It's all of ours. It belongs to us all. It belongs to the students who will take charge of their own education. It belongs to the principals who will develop procedures and programs to benefit the students. It belongs to the other teachers on my team and the resource teachers that collectively educate all of the students. It belongs to the maintenance and sanitation staff that provide unbelievable facilities for all of us to use. It belongs to the parents who entrust all of these people to educate their children. And yes, it belongs to me, just as it belonged to me when I was just a young student volunteering to help out. What is more exciting than having my own room and developing my own lessons is working alongside all of these incredible stakeholders and professional colleagues. For me personally, it's a childhood dream come true that I am working alongside my mentor and friend, the teacher who inspired me to actually join this profession at the beginning of my 6th grade year. These people are the reason I wake up at 5 o'clock every morning with a smile on my face.

So, here's the deal. The great thing about teachers, the really good ones, is that their curriculum could be the alphabet or differential calculus and it wouldn't change how they teach their students and their ultimate goal. The good ones help you figure out who you are. They help you learn about your strengths and how to be happy and successful in your life. I was lucky enough to meet one of these teachers with that "it" factor, those responsive dispositions that make a difference in students' lives. Mrs. Huffman taught me how to be a student, how to love learning, and how to have an unquenchable passion for giving back what she gave to me. I spent every year after the 6th grade volunteering as much time as humanly possible in her classroom. In high school it was every teacher workday and my exam days. In my early college years it became my days without classes and holiday break. Throughout all of this time I was developing a sense of comfort and belonging in the classroom and in front of students. I was learning how to be a teacher in the most traditional sense of the word. I learned how to instruct, manage a classroom, and build relationships with the students. However, the most important thing I learned was how to be a teacher who respects and cherishes opportunities to collaborate with other teachers, gain new and different perspectives, and to share the responsibility of an education with all of those who are to benefit from that education, t.

Mrs. Huffman didn't spend all of those extra hours with me because it made her look good or because she had something to gain. Mrs. Huffman did it because she understood. She understood that this is what makes good teachers. She had that hard to find quality, and she saw it in me. I should be calling her Brooke; she's trying to get me to call her by her first name now that we work together. But that's the thing about teachers that inspire you and teachers that really teach you, about life, and yourself, and how to be invested in your own education; they will always be your teacher. They never stop. She'll always be Mrs. Huffman who is my partner in my education.

It's easier said than done, being inclusive as professional educator. The system is somewhat stacked against this concept. The public school is set up as a hierarchy. At the top of your ladder you have your school board, then superintendent, assistant superintendents, department directors, principals, assistant principals, teachers, and finally students. It seems natural to think, well, the students report to the teachers, the teachers to the principals, and so on. That makes sense right? The students wouldn't behave and do their work if the teachers didn't force them. The teachers would show movies and flex the curriculum, if principals don't check up on them. Right? That actually is right if we all choose to live by and agree with the hierarchy. But who does this hierarchy really help? I understand the need to be accountable to people, and that this accountability can help maintain that the stakeholders have a high level of quality. However, it also cultivates an environment where not everyone is an equal participant in the education of students. It creates a culture where people feel like they have to impress and grandstand in order to look good to the people above them on the ladder. It creates an environment of selfish behavior and makes the educational process about "me" and not "us."

As a teacher, my thoughts don't revolve around impressing my principal. They revolve around my students and doing everything I can to educate and thus empower them. However, it can be hard to keep this mindset within a hierarchical system. It's hard to keep your head down and focus, when everything around you is screaming to keep looking up. But it's the students, down at the bottom of the ladder, that stand to have the most to gain or lose from what everyone above them does. Doesn't that mean that they should be the biggest stakeholders and the biggest contributors to their own education? When teachers work together, and principals work with teachers, and all of these people actually work with students and their parents, we all succeed, and we all grow. Students don't need an authoritative teacher to stand up in front of the class and tell them what's in their best interest and tell them what to think and what to do. They need a teacher who will care enough about them to give them opportunities and guide them to learn. That's all it is, giving opportunities. I give my students chances to succeed and fail and to learn from those failures. I give them chances to rise above what's expected. My students have to take hold of their own education and take responsibility for it as well. To me, that is the only way to ensure that they keep growing and learning once they leave me.

Part of the struggle to fight the hierarchy is the attitude that, "This is my classroom. I don't want anyone else coming in and telling me what to do." Teachers with the "it" factor don't get territorial for the wrong reasons. They do care about the quality of teaching that happens in their school, and they do care about giving the best of themselves and others to the students. They are eager and willing to share their classroom and students with other educators who share their professionalism. I always want the EC Resource teacher on my team to look at my lessons and activities and make suggestions and changes. I am always eager to have the ELL Teacher come into my classroom and help me reach all of my students. I want my colleagues input and help. It isn't *my* classroom. They aren't *my* students. It's all of ours. They are all of ours. Teaching is most effective when teachers work together and make learning interdisciplinary and cohesive. Students only stand to gain when their education seems relevant and important no matter whose classroom they are in, or who is in my classroom. It only helps when they see that there is a whole team of adults who care about them and that are working together to help them succeed. It can be hard to be open and receptive to everyone's input on what you do. However, we are all professionals and part of being a professional is taking a step back to consider all of the necessary pieces in the puzzle of teaching.

I'm not going to pretend that I haven't had to work incredibly hard and learn a whole lot to be the kind of teacher that I am. I'm not so naive as to think that anything about teaching is easy. However, there are certain things that just kind of come naturally. It's that thing, that quality, the dispositions that we are talking about. It's incredibly hard to learn, not impossible, but incredibly hard. Some people just have it. Some teachers are naturally inclusive. They are inclusive of their colleagues and their students. They inherently understand the importance of being unified and equal, as opposed to hierarchical.

I like to think I am naturally disposed to be professionally inclusive, but there are some things that I have learned that help me maintain this type of professionalism. That's what being inclusive is; it's professional. Teachers are professionals who have a certain set of skills and knowledge, just like doctors and lawyers. When good doctors are working on making the best decision for a patient, and when good lawyers are trying to figure out the best way to argue a case in court, they don't lock themselves in a room and work alone. They find ways to collaborate to figure out the best solution. They talk to their patients and clients. They talk to their colleagues to get another professional opinion. Good teachers do the same thing. Their students need to be actively involved in the education and their colleagues do as well. So, here's what I've learned about how to be a professional:

1 Everyone is different. Everyone is an individual.
   This includes students and teachers. The things that engage one student in their education isn't going to engage someone else. I have to learn who my students are and when they feel empowered. I inquire about their lives and interests. I ask for their feedback on their education. I give them guidelines and opportunities and allow them to be creative in how they present their understanding to me. I also have to understand that the way I communicate and negotiate with one colleague isn't the best way to do it with another. Some of my teammates need me to be blunt and to the point, and others need me to be more appeasing and diplomatic. I have to learn who my colleagues are and how I can work with them. Some educators make a mistake by focusing on what students and teachers need to do in order to work with

them. They should direct that focus on themselves. I can only control what I can control, and what I can control is how *I* can better work with others.

2 I have to make it a priority.

It is easy to get caught up in all of the other things that come along with being a teacher. It is easy to get busy and make lessons that I like and that work for me. It is easy to fall into my place in the hierarchy and make things simpler, but it is my job to fight the easy. It is my job to work hard, harder than any of us get recognition for, but do it anyway. I have to make a point to set up meetings with support staff and team teachers to talk about and reflect on our practices. I have to make a point of thinking about every single student when I make my lesson plans. If that means that I have 100 different variations of my lesson, then that is what I do. I have to make it my greatest priority to empower the students to do the learning themselves and not do the work for them, even if that would be easier.

3 I have to stand up for my profession.

I have to be okay with fighting against a system that is fundamentally ingrained in most of us. The hierarchy isn't exactly natural to all of us, but it is definitely societal. It can be difficult to go against the grain and be different, but our profession needs us to do just that. Educating shouldn't be administrative or political; it should be personal and purposeful. I have to stand up for what I believe teachers should do and what should be done for teachers in order for us to truly be able to include everyone in our process.

4 It's a gift. Don't waste it.

5 This thing, this "it" factor, it's a gift. It's truly a blessing and gift from the world that I get to do what I do, and that I have what it takes to make a difference. Not everybody has it. I wasn't blessed with that athletic factor to be a pro basketball player. I wasn't graced with that taste factor to be chef. I wasn't honored with the eye for art and design. I got the "it" factor for teaching. I can't squander that amazing power by not sharing it. I need to give some of my power to my students and my co-workers. I need to be a Mrs. Huffman to my students, even if it's just one kid that I reach. I need to break the cycle that tells students they have no choice or stake in their education. I need to break the cycle that tells teachers to shut their doors and do what they do. If you have "it," or even if you are still developing "it," if you have decided to be a part of this wonderful, frustrating, exhilarating profession, don't waste it.

Looking back, I remember walking into school the Monday before the first day to go and meet my new 6th grade teacher. I love being at school. I love the smells and the people. I love coming up with spelling sheets and helping grade my mom's papers. I have been waiting all summer to spend my last free days in the empty building doing "teacher things." I love it. Nothing compares.

"Hey," I say in a low voice, face red. "I have you this year."

"Hello! Okay now what's your name?"

"Kalie."

She smiled, "I'm Mrs. Huffman."

So, why are you here? What is it that made you want to do this? What is it that is special about you, your "it" factor? It's something elusive that good teachers are. Good teachers have it because they are here for the reasons that they should be here. They want to put in the extra work to be inclusive. They care too much not to do it. That is the bottom line. I care too much not to give 110% every day for every student, teacher, parent, principal, director, custodian, community member, and myself. It's in me. It's who I am. That's why I'm here.

PART 3

Just Do It: *Processes and Tools*

..

CHAPTER 13

Using DIA: Breaking it Down

Think about:

1 Do you know teachers that you would consider to have responsive
   dispositions? Do you know ones that you would consider technically
   disposed?
2 What type of evidence would you use to support your conclusions?

• • •

Let's practice assessing teachers' *Dispositions in Action*. The following vignettes
come from earlier studies of *Dispositions in Action* over time. I was able to
observe and interview five teachers over the course of six years. A comparison
was done of the teachers' dispositions in student teaching, their first year of
teaching, and their fifth year of teaching. Vignettes designed from the final
year of the study follow. As you read each classroom snapshot, think about the
following questions.

How and where are responsive dispositions evidenced? How and where are
dispositions that are technical evidenced?

Jot down notes or make tally marks when you see evidence of:

Responsive assessment	Technical assessment	Responsive instruction	Technical instruction	Responsive management	Technical management
Critical	Assuming	Facilitative	Directing	Empowering	Controlling
Challenging	Accepting	Creative	Repetitive	Connected	Distanced:

© KONINKLIJKE BRILL NV, LEIDEN, 2018 | DOI 10.1163/9789004364486_013

1   **Vignette One: Language Arts Classroom**

Caitlyn's classroom is a journey into stories of the past and connections to present issues of equity as the lessons center on "racism, boycotts and freedom writers." The learning goals for the class are posted on the whiteboard, noting the aspects of studying nonfiction and the correlated state Language Arts standards. After reading several nonfiction books and articles about our nation's struggles with issues of race, social class, and gender, the class explores how these have been present throughout our nation's history. The whole class discusses how our government and society have dealt with these concerns, with a focus on rights and laws. The students and the teacher ask questions and share experiences that help them begin to connect historical events to more contemporary ones. The teacher asks students if they would like to share their own experiences with issues of equity and race and engages students in focused conversation at their tables and then brings the conversation back to the whole class. Table groups informally share and interact with each other, building on each other's responses and asking more in depth questions.

The class has brainstormed a list of famous events that have occurred in our society and their resulting consequences framed by themes of love, hatred and racism. The teacher makes connections back to their prior thinking and poses a question for students to examine. She leads them through a discussion of what actions undertaken by the people involved seemed to advance their goals for change and what seemed to make it more difficult. The students decide that peaceful resistance seems to have helped the most. The teacher pushes them to justify their choices and talk about why. Issues of race and gender are openly and calmly discussed with the students listening and offering their thoughts to the teacher and one another.

The desks are arranged into tables with sets of four desks pulled together so students may face each other and interact. The agenda for the double block class period is posted as SSR, Writer's Workshop, and a nonfiction book discussion and activity related to the topics at hand. School-wide rules about being prepared, raising hands, and remaining seated are posted on the wall, indicating inappropriate behavior. They are followed by a range of consequences as students accumulate "strikes" for misbehavior, but the students and teacher do not even seem to notice or need their presence as basic reminders about community as other people's perspectives and needs are organically cultivated through instruction and discussion. The teacher later shared in her five years of teaching she has had to send a student to the office for a referral only four times. Usually a look is all that is needed. Occasionally, the teacher refocuses the group as they begin to discuss amongst themselves, but they are quick to come back into the groups' discussions when it is time.

The teacher asks about other groups who may have been struggling with attaining rights in our country. The class quickly responds "women." There is discussion about women's roles now and in the past as the teacher asks students what they know. She uses this to guide her further instruction. The students begin eagerly chiming in with questions about why there were all white, male juries (and are there still?). They express concern about single mothers in the past who did not have land rights and how they would take care of their children. They make other connections and shift the focus to men asking for a girl's hand in marriage.

Next, a video clip about Susan B. Anthony from the Discovery Channel is pulled up on the SmartBoard and students seem very interested, watching quietly. They have been told they will be using the ideas in the clip for a team activity exploring women's rights shortly after. Their homework will be continued work from their Writer's Workshop in the form of a memoir related to their own experiences with any of the issues that had framed the class for the past few days, guided by a rubric.

2   Vignette Two: Math and Science Classroom

Debbie's classroom centers on understanding through doing. The focus is on helping students make connections to Math and Science by using their own words, thoughts, and experiences whenever possible and making the needed "chores" of the classroom fun through interactive games and assignments. Today they are reviewing for a test by playing "Energy Jeopardy." Students sit at tables and work together to determine answers to the game, helping each other work out the needed Math processes and formulas. They know that the table group that collaborates the best and works hard to find the correct answers is always rewarded with the best group totem, which is passed from group to group, along with a treat bag to honor their success.

After the game, students return to work on their Science projects, which require them to create a headline and related story about an energy/environmental issue of their choice. The assignment needs to demonstrate their understanding of the chosen topic and work toward helping to address the situation by informing and persuading others. The students talk while they work, seeking to make their stories both interesting and visually appealing to each other.

When they are finished, they come up to get an article about "brown outs" and are told to use a highlighter to indicate what they deem important within the text, a skill with which they seem both confident and familiar.

3   **Vignette Three: Language Arts Classroom**

Amy's classroom runs smoothly as the students know what to do, pretty much on their own. The focus is on a calm and friendly atmosphere governed by clear procedures and processes that help students complete activities and assignments in an efficient and involved manner. Tools to help the classroom run smoothly and to help students make appropriate behavior choices are in place. Agendas are signed focusing students on tasks that need to be completed, reward cards are signed to keep students focused and on task, and teacher created classroom rules and related punishments, or "consequences," are posted on the wall. Procedures for students to use the classroom sets of trade books are also clearly posted, instructing students how to check out books, to make sure they read the ENTIRE book and then complete the computerized test on the book. Students are seated in a double row "U" shape so that the teacher can see all of them and redirect as needed.

The daily goals for this Language Arts classroom are posted on the board in the form of a content objective from the state standard course of study, along with the day's activities, which include a vocabulary crossword, a scavenger hunt, and a vocabulary writing assignment. As the students enter the class, they are told to tuck in their shirts, zip their jackets, and to get quiet before they come into the classroom. Students, after some quiet talking, get seated. The first part of the class is spent on silent reading time. A timer is set and students begin to read. The teacher circulates around the room to do on the spot conferences in which the students must tell her who the antagonist and protagonist in their books are and why they choose each person. Conferences last about three minutes and occur in hushed whispers. After about 15 minutes, the timer goes off and students are told to write down the number of pages they read in their logs.

Next, students go over their vocabulary crossword by being called upon one at a time and asked to tell the class answers and definitions. Students need to listen as they may be called on without volunteering, sometimes prior to the question being asked. Reinforcement and feedback is given in the form of "good" and "not quite" as the teacher explains incorrect responses. As new vocabulary words are discussed, the teacher asks students for definitions as she offers up her own personal examples, which were also used in the previous class. The teacher uses a courtroom example to define "object," a three-legged dog to illustrate "atypical," and states that snakes are creatures for which she has "antipathy." Once this is done, the crosswords are collected so that students get credit for their completion.

Next the students engage in a vocabulary definition copying game, where they work with a teacher chosen partner to walk around the room, looking at words and covered definitions under flaps to find matching words and definitions and then copy them down. Directions are continually stressed and repeated to help students stay on task and accomplish their goal. It appears to be a contest to see who can get done first. This goes on for about 35 minutes, with the teacher circulating among groups and giving them hints and answers when they get the words and definitions confused.

Before the students leave, the teacher walks around the room signing agendas and reward cards. Students are told about their "challenging" homework assignment. They are given a list of 12 vocabulary words in sets of three. They must use each of these three words in one sentence and it "has to make sense." The students calmly exit the classroom at the end of the period.

4   Vignette Four: Math Classroom

Janet's classroom is all about doing the right thing. This is fostered by understanding the teacher's expectations, knowing Math content and procedures, and getting rewards for hard work. Helping students out with intervention when they don't "get it" is a big part of the classroom emphasis. Practice is used to reinforce student proficiency, along with one-on-one student/teacher support and after school tutoring. Benchmark tests are used to note students' progress, but the use of ongoing informal assessments, such as whiteboards to work out math problems and indicate students' visual responses (thumbs up or down), help the teacher to know when students need more support. Students get rewards (recess time, fun math games, etc.) after they meet baseline Math competency expectations and are ready to move ahead.

Students sit in neat, closely structured rows with their attention directed to the front of the room. Reminders about school and classrooms rules, expectations, and consequences are clearly present and referred to by the teacher when needed. The students get out their homework and work on a "bell work" problem posted on the board as the teacher walks around, checking and recording who has completed their homework assignments. Students work quietly and individually. Janet announces that the other classes had more completed homework assignments and are moving closer to winning the "free day" next Friday. She reminds them that everyone in the class needs to have homework completed if they want to win this coveted prize.

The teacher then goes over the correct way to do the "bell work" and asks students if they have any questions. There are none. She then has them open the textbook to the new assignment for the day. She uses examples to go over needed steps and procedures using the overhead projector. Then she writes a problem down for students to solve. The students work out the problems on their white boards and hold them up so she can check to see who is getting it right and with whom she needs to go over it again. Next, the students begin independent practice on the new work as the teacher walks around giving individual help to those who need it. They all successfully "work hard" and keep focused so they can play a fun Math game for the last ten minutes of class. The game begins, and students work individually to get answers and then accumulate team points. They are focused and relatively quiet during the game, though the teacher reminds them about the class losing Friday freeday points if they get too wound up.

At the end of class, students have the teacher sign their homework logs to show their parents what the new work is for tonight. She gently reminds six of the students that they will be coming to work with her for remediation at lunch so they can get their test scores up. She knows they can do it!

5   **Vignette Five: Science Classroom**

Sarah's Science classroom is a place of engaged discovery. The teacher allows students to decide how and why to set up labs to examine the day's essential question. They need to figure out what should be the dependent, independent, or controlled variables. The teacher offers support by continually asking why they made specific choices related to both the content and how they are going to show what they learn. Sarah informally explains her own pedagogical and management choices, telling students why she is doing what she is doing as a natural part of classroom dialogue. This acts both as a model for the students to consider their own choices and to allow students to see the legitimacy of the rules and procedures for their lab work.

Desks are clustered into groups and classical music plays quietly in the background. Students are working on a lab they have set up as decided through discussion and a decision making process that will enable them to consider which natural resources are most valuable and why they think so. They examine samples and negotiate understandings about the resource sample with their lab team. They then work to determine what makes a substance more or less valuable. They record their teams' decisions and findings on the Smartboard for later whole class comparisons.

The "essential question" for the day is posted on the board. As students work with the teacher to design their lab, they explain to the teacher how the decisions and processes they will be using in class demonstrate the essential question, giving it meaning and life. There are no rules posted on the wall, but instead a list of desired learner characteristics and outcomes such as students becoming "thinkers, principled, risk takers, caring, knowledgeable, open-minded and reflective." If students get off task or need redirection, the teacher refers them to their lab guide (constructed with and by students), which articulates approaches, behaviors and attitudes needed to work effectively as inquirers. The classroom hums with busy talk, but when the teacher needs the focus of the whole class, she asks for their eyes and ears or counts down from three to one, prompting them to become quiet and attentive. If students have trouble answering the open-ended questions within their lab work or giving a class response, she asks them if they would like to choose someone to help them out. This allows students to guide each other to understanding as they clarify what they mean and offer alternative examples that build on one another's responses. Humor and smiles are present as the teacher crafts the lab with students as they recall where they left off in the lab preparation from the last class and get busy. As students work in teams of three on their lab, the teacher circulates, encouraging them to "make your argument for your conclusions" and to engage in "intense discussions while listening to and respecting other viewpoints"

Students continue with their Science lab to explore the value of natural resources. They talk throughout, making their points of view, thoughts about the resources, and their value clear to one another. The classical music continues to play in the background for student enjoyment and as a reminder to keep the discussions and deliberations at a conversational level. As they examine the resource samples, argue their points within their teams, and record their data, team representatives know to walk up to the Smartboard to record their choices for class analysis and discussion.

Think again:

1 Which teacher seems to be the most responsive overall?
2 Compare whether teachers tend to be more or less responsive when it comes to assessment, instruction, or management? Is there a trend that cuts across the vignettes? Why do you think that is so?
3 Use the Responsive DIA Observation Scale (below) for each teacher. How did your initial thoughts and responses compare to your scores on the DIA Observation Scale?
4 How was your group's inter-rater reliability? Do you feel ready to observe and determine levels of responsive dispositions in other teacher's classrooms? How can you get better at doing this?

Compare your notes and scores to the research findings:
Try using your field notes (jotted down or tallied up earlier) to rate the teachers' level of responsive *Dispositions in Action* using the following observation scale.

TABLE 13.1   *Responsive DIA Observation.*

Responsive interaction within assessment (challenging/critical)			
Indicators of dispositions via dialogue high level of responsiveness (3)	Indicators of dispositions via dialogue medium level of responsiveness (2)	Indicators of dispositions via dialogue low level of responsiveness (1)	Score/ comments
Expectations: The teacher regularly talks with students and interacts with them in ways that authentically communicate high expectations for learning.	*Expectations:* The teacher indicates that some students are capable of meeting high expectations while others are not as capable.	*Expectations:* The teacher talks with students and interacts with them in ways that emphasize effort and compliance as success.	
Understanding: Dialogue and interaction regularly encourage deeper levels of understanding and emphasize progress toward high quality performances of understanding.	*Understanding:* Dialogue and interaction go beyond the "givens" of the task toward higher levels of thinking.	*Understanding:* Dialogue and interaction focus on completion of tasks and assignments with little probing or questioning to move beyond the "givens" of the task.	

Responsive interaction within assessment (challenging/critical)

Indicators of dispositions via dialogue high level of responsiveness (3)	Indicators of dispositions via dialogue medium level of responsiveness (2)	Indicators of dispositions via dialogue low level of responsiveness (1)	Score/comments
Questioning: Dialogue and interaction focus on questioning and probing to reveal the students' depth of understanding to move beyond surface assumptions and statements of "facts," often seeking students' opinions, or justifications and reasoning behind responses.	*Questioning:* Dialogue and interactions typically center on teacher questions that focus on seeking the correct answer to a question or set of questions, with occasional follow up to check for student understanding.	*Questioning:* Dialogue and interaction center on the teacher typically providing information, with limited focus on questioning students or student questions.	
Methods of assessment: Assessment of learning (both formative and summative) occurs regularly within the flow of student/student/teacher interactions throughout instruction and is used to set goals for students and to guide further learning.	*Methods of assessment:* Assessment of learning occurs in pre-determined projects, activities or assignments and is primarily of a summative nature, with occasional informal checks for understanding.	*Methods of assessment:* Assessment takes place almost exclusively separate form instruction (usually post) using methods such as tests and quizzes.	

TABLE 13.1   *Responsive DIA Observation.*

Responsive interaction within instruction (facilitative/creative)

Indicators of dispositions via dialogue high level (3)	Indicators of dispositions via dialogue medium level (2)	Indicators of dispositions via dialogue low level (1)	Score/comments
Individualization: The teacher frequently responds to student questions, notes their progress, and incorporates their ideas, experiences and interests into instruction.	*Individualization:* The teacher responds to student questions, progress, and ideas and occasionally builds this into instruction.	*Individualization:* The teacher emphasizes one approach to learning for all students.	
Conceptual understanding: Lessons regularly feature the scaffolding of skills and concepts to build on students' current understanding and questions to obtain deeper levels of understanding including synthesis and evaluation	*Conceptual understanding:* Lessons occasionally vary the explanation of concepts and the performance of skills in response to students' questions, typically focused an application level of understanding.	*Conceptual understanding:* Lessons emphasize the explanation of concepts in a prescribed order typically focused on a recall level of understanding.	
Developmental responsiveness: The teacher talks and interacts with students in ways that indicate responsiveness to individual differences in developmental needs.	*Developmental responsiveness:* The teacher talks and interacts with students in ways that show some awareness of individual differences in developmental needs.	*Developmental responsiveness:* The teacher talks with students and interacts with them in ways that are not developmentally responsive and are often the same from class to class and situation to situation and student to student.	

Responsive interaction within instruction (facilitative/creative)

Indicators of dispositions via dialogue high level (3)	Indicators of dispositions via dialogue medium level (2)	Indicators of dispositions via dialogue low level (1)	Score/comments
Relevance: The teacher regularly relates classroom learning experiences to real world situations and makes connections to students' lives beyond school.	*Relevance:* The teacher occasionally relates classroom learning experiences to real world situations and makes connections to students' lives beyond school.	*Relevance:* The teacher talks with students and interacts with them in ways that emphasize the coverage of information. Any connections beyond the classroom are incidental.	
Multiple paths to understanding: The teacher encourages multiple ways of demonstrating depth of understanding within and after instruction	*Multiple paths to understanding:* The teacher offers may offer multiple opportunities for student demonstration of understanding primarily after instruction.	*Multiple paths to understanding:* The teacher emphasizes a single pathway to learning and assessing whether or not students demonstrate prescribed skills and procedures after instruction.	
Feedback: The teacher regularly provides multiple forms of feedback to students to guide the growth of their understanding during instruction, building on and challenging students' conceptual understanding.	*Feedback:* The teacher occasionally provides feedback to students during instruction, primarily focused on addressing students' misconceptions.	*Feedback:* The teacher generally limits feedback to grades on assignments, with only corrective feedback during instruction.	

TABLE 13.1   *Responsive DIA Observation.*

Responsive interaction with students (empowering/connected)

Indicators of dispositions via dialogue high level (3)	Indicators of dispositions via dialogue medium level (2)	Indicators of dispositions via dialogue low level (1)	Score/comments
Decision making: The teacher regularly seeks input from students related to instructional strategies, assessment and the focus of the curriculum and instruction in the classroom.	*Decision making:* The teacher occasionally involves students in instructional decisions by giving options within assignments or projects.	*Decision making:* The teacher focuses on covering information and material with very few adjustments made related to student feedback or input.	
Curriculum and instruction: The teacher elicits student questions and interpretation of learning to gain data to inform future plans related to aspects of classroom curriculum and instruction.	*Curriculum and instruction:* The teacher gives students some choices about what to learn and how to learn.	*Curriculum and instruction:* The teacher rarely seeks feedback from students related to curriculum and instruction.	
Classroom expectations: Structure and organization in classroom supports dialogue and interaction with individuals and groups of students in running the classroom.	*Classroom expectations:* Students have some choices regarding classroom procedures.	*Classroom expectations:* The teacher talks with students and interacts with them in ways that emphasize following directions, rules and completing tasks.	

Responsive interaction with students (empowering/connected)

Indicators of dispositions via dialogue high level (3)	Indicators of dispositions via dialogue medium level (2)	Indicators of dispositions via dialogue low level (1)	Score/comments
Student rapport: Student dialogue with each other and teacher is truly collaborative with a focus on quality and mutual support in setting and attaining goals and personal support.	*Student rapport:* Classroom conversations indicate a congenial, cooperative atmosphere with some student interaction to achieve learning goals	*Student rapport:* Teacher talk rarely veers from focus on "given" content and coverage of this content with limited student interaction.	
Individual management: The teacher talks with students and interacts with them in ways that show "withitness" and keen awareness of individual students, and flexibility in responding to each student.	*Individual management:* The teacher talks with students and interacts with them in ways that show some awareness of individual differences and some variation in responding to students.	*Individual management:* The teacher talks with students and interacts with them in ways that center on maintaining consistency and authority in responding to students.	
Classroom management: The teacher proactively addresses disruptions and promotes student engagement in ways that encourage shared responsibility and a sense of community and intrinsic motivation. The focus is on student problem solving.	*Classroom management:* The teacher addresses disruptions and promotes student engagement in ways that primarily emphasize extrinsic motivation. The focus is on "on task" behavior.	*Classroom management:* Teacher addresses disruptions and promotes engagement in primarily autocratic ways, The focus is on individual compliance with class rules and norms.	

(From Thornton & Strahan, 2004)

This tool is premised on the following assertions related to dispositions:

1   A basic dictionary definition of "disposition" is "one's customary frame of mind." For educational purposes we define dispositions as "teacher's habits of mind that shape ways that they interact with students and the ways they make decisions in the classroom."
2   Dispositions are evidenced through interaction with students and the kinds of dialogue observed in the classrooms.
3   Scores are between 3.0–1.0 with varying degrees including 3.0, 2.75, 2.5, 2.0, 1.75, 1.5, 1.0

6   What Did We Find?

You may choose to average the scores to get an overall rating or level of responsive dispositions. Caitlyn and Sarah consistently evidenced level three dispositions. Debbie and Amy's scores fall into the level two range. Janet's overall average score would be a 1.5, as she exhibits level one in some domains and two in others.

A comparison of the observation comments and scores to some of their interview responses helps to check for our interpretation and consider face validity of our results.

7   Interview Data

Caitlyn "Tell me about your classroom management."

> Well, student engagement is probably the most important aspect of classroom management. If students are engaged in what they are doing, whether it be reading, writing, or projects, there is not going to be a problem with classroom management. I have found that when my students are connected to what they are doing, they work harder and genuinely care about the final product. I have found that respect is the most important thing to gain from students. If they know you respect them as a person, then they will return the same respect to you.

The focus on connection, caring, and reciprocal respect shows her responsive disposition.

"What do you value the most in terms of assessment?"

> *This is a tough one. I know without a doubt what the most important aspect of student assessment is, but I can't say that it is what I do. Student assessment should be relevant and authentic. However, with state mandated testing, and a school system that is test-driven, relevant and authentic testing gets tossed to the wayside.... Before I started teaching, I would have answered that the most important aspect would be that an assessment show whether or not a student 'gets it.' But now, after 4 years of teaching, I would say that an assessment is there to help students practice for the EOG. You teach a concept, test, then move on to the next one.... I will have to say that I do use authentic assessment on a daily basis. ... I listen to the students to determine if they are getting it.*

She exhibits a level three responsive disposition in her observation, even related to assessment, but she also describes the challenges she faces in enacting that disposition.

Debbie

Debbie had moved to another rural school during her second year of teaching. In her interview responses, she talked about how this school had a healthier atmosphere and how the teachers had more freedom to do what is "best for kids." Now that she was in this new setting, she could continue to work toward instruction that was engaging, inquiry-based, and real world focused as well as to use multiple forms of assessing students.

> *Since my students are kind of high risk and have trouble with testing, getting them really involved and letting them show me in different ways what they are learning is important. It may be games that serve as a more traditional review for tests they have to take, or activities and projects to really get them involved.*

When asked, "Tell me about your professional relationships with administrators and other teachers," she talked about how she was teaching in a place where perhaps there is not strong administrative leadership, but where teachers can kind of "do their own thing."

Her level two responsive dispositions are evidenced in the observation. She often demonstrates a responsive disposition with a technical twist to make sure students are "doing and getting what they need."

Amy

"What is important to you when you think about your classroom instruction?"

> *It is important that students keep engaged in learning so that they can understand and retain it, but they also need to know what is expected of them and get the work done. You can't give them too much freedom or they may get off-track.*

Her assessment focused heavily on making sure students did well on end of grade and writing tests, but she also talked about the need for students to read real books and have a chance to respond to them. She spoke of this tension between responsive and technical thinking and action in her professional interactions as well.

> *The principal really likes me, so I get to do some things that are a little different, as long as my test scores are okay and I show that I am doing what I need to do, and then I can try to do more things that are fun and exciting for the students.*

Her focus was on compliance, but she expressed a desire to work toward change.

Throughout Amy's interview, she indicated both responsive and technical dispositions in all domains. She believed that it was important for students to have a voice in the classroom, but she embedded this heavily within the teacher's pre-determined rules and procedures. She had very specific classroom procedures to follow and relied heavily on extrinsic rewards and praise to get students to follow directions. In terms of instruction, she wanted to keep students engaged and thinking, but not asking too many questions. She stressed they should act like "good workers." Her overall level two dispositions are evidenced as she seeks to balance the technical and responsive in her decisions and interactions.

Janet

Janet's interview was consistent with the observed evidence of technical dispositions (level one responsiveness) in the areas of student interactions/management and assessment. When asked about management she stated:

> *The most important aspects of classroom management are fairness, communication, consistency, and the quickness in which you respond to inappropriate action. Students need to know that you respect them and will treat them with fairness if they act inappropriately in the classroom. In addition to fairness, students need to know your expectations ahead of*

time, and they need to know what appropriate behavior looks like. I usually take a little bit of time at the beginning of the year to visually show them what I expect to see in my classroom. Every time we do something different or an activity, I go over what my expectations are and what I should not see. Students need to know your consequences like calling home or staying for detention. I have also found that the quickness in which I respond to something is important...sometimes students don't even realize what they were doing, and they need to know immediately that whatever it was needs to stop. Good behavior needs to be noticed and rewarded though. It needs to be made attractive so that others will also want to partake in doing things right. A simple homework pass to everyone who turned their assignment in on time is a quick and easy and FREE way to reward your students.

When asked about assessment, she focused primarily on student performance, contextualized by testing.

The most important aspects of student assessment are that it is meaningful and that you do something with it. Students need to see how they performed on something, understand where they made mistakes, and be given some remediation time in order to master the material. Student assessments also need to be communicated to someone at home. Authentic assessment is, of course, the best but can't always be the only option (especially in such a tested subject like math).

Her responses related to instruction focused on student mastery of learning and getting things right, but she tried to weave in some active learning and fun, indicating level two responsiveness.

Usually, I take a small amount of time to introduce something new, give them an opportunity to try it with someone, and then, of course, to try it on their own. After some basic mastery has taken place, we do some sort of activity/game/moving around the room thing to build on what we learned. Sometimes students need help connecting previous knowledge to what they just learned, but it amazes me to see how confident they become when they realize that they already had the knowledge to complete the problem. My ultimate goal in instruction is for it to never be boring or mundane. I always want class to be exciting and fun mixed with learning.

Her interview exhibits a more technical, level one, responsiveness. She focuses on doing what she is told rather than questioning these "duties" and working for change, as she saw this as doing what was best for her students.

Professionalism is adhering to the duties and roles expected of oneself as defined by their chosen profession. As a teacher, I enact professionalism by completing the duties expected of me at my school; bus duty, attending faculty meetings, being a participant at curriculum meetings, and by furthering my own learning. I am a professional because I do what I do to the best of my ability. I don't take shortcuts or try to shortchange my students.

Sarah

Sarah had been teaching Science in the same middle school for five years. Her interview responses reflect a high three level of responsive dispositions, as does her observation. Her responses related to interactions with students focused on caring and understanding the cause of any problems students may have, so that she can help them work to solve these problems. In terms of assessment, Sarah stated, *"The focus is on developing the depth, the level of their understanding, definitely NOT grades."*

She stated, *"I am a facilitator. I assist my students in learning the information for themselves. To do this, I ask them questions to get them thinking, or help to direct their path if they get lost."*

When talking about professional relationships, her first focus was on students.

With the students it means caring, but as a parent would—helping, listening, and keeping confidences when appropriate. It also includes taking care of yourself and continuing your own education so that you can provide the best for your students. With other teachers, professionalism would be more like a neighbor. Meaning we are respectful, helpful, and open-minded, while at the same time still holding each other accountable for always working to the benefit of the students. With administrators and parents, I believe you need to have an open line of communication about anything that affects students. This would include honesty and speaking up even when it is hard. Additionally, with administration, it would involve following rules/guidelines that are in place while at the same time working to change rules/guidelines that you do not believe benefit students.

8   DIA Results

As indicated on the DIA observation scale, an exact "score" might fall in between

identified levels; therefore, the use of decimals may be helpful depending

	Student interactions	Instruction interactions	Assessment interactions	Professional interactions
Interview	3	3	3	3
Observation	3	3	3	N/O

on the purpose of the assessment. For the purposes of this demonstration, I

	Student interactions	Instruction interactions	Assessment interactions	Professional interactions
Interview	2	2	2	2
Observation	2	2	2	N/O

chose to focus exclusively on using a score of one, two, or three, reporting the

	Student interactions	Instruction interactions	Assessment interactions	Professional interactions
Interview	2	2	2	2
Observation	2	2	2	N/O

score that was most prevalent within each domain.

	Student interactions	Instruction interactions	Assessment interactions	Professional interactions
Interview	1	2	1	1
Observation	1	1	1	N/O

Caitlyn   *responsive disposition level (1–3)*

	Student interactions	Instruction interactions	Assessment interactions	Professional interactions
Interview	3	3	3	3
Observation	3	3	3	N/O

Amy   *responsive disposition level (1–3)*
Debbie   *responsive disposition level (1–3)*
Janet   *responsive disposition level (1–3)*
Sarah   *responsive disposition level (1–3)*

The process of observing, analyzing and rating an educator's *Dispositions in Action* can give insight to teachers and others into the dispositions they possess and demonstrate in their teaching. It may further allow a comparison between teachers' goals for student learning and their instructional and relational decisions. They can then set dispositional development goals to become the type of teachers they hope to be.

Reference

Thornton, H., & Strahan, D. (2004). *Dispositions in action observation scale*. Greensboro, NC: University of North Carolina.

The It Factor Tool Kit

Think about:

1 What tools are currently used to assess teachers?
2 What do they reveal (about the teacher, the school, the student, the community, legislative mandates)?

•••

The assessment of educator *Dispositions in Action* can lead to meaningful discussions and serve multiple purposes in terms of developing a professional community of teachers. The fact that *Dispositions in Action* center on dispositions as evidenced in classroom interactions and related student learning enables teachers and administrators to move beyond a conceptual discussion of dispositions. There is concrete evidence of how teachers' dispositions affect decisions made about the nature of student learning through interactions as pedagogical choices. It may also open up other discussions related to what type of learning are we emphasizing in our classrooms and creating for or with our students. Practically, the use of the *Dispositions in Action* model allows teachers and administrators to reflect upon individual practice and potential professional development related to dispositions. It further engenders discussion of one's educational philosophy, the congruence of that philosophy with educational decisions in the classroom, and its alignment with overall learning goals. The ultimate question to begin examining one's dispositions may be "What changes do I want to see in my students after spending a year in my classroom?" and why.

1   DIA for Administrators and Human Resource Departments

One of the hardest and most important decisions made within the educational arena is who should become a new member of a school community. Hiring the right teacher is important, but it is not often easy. Reviewing candidate resumes, speaking with references (who are likely going to be as positive as possible), and interviewing are the most likely steps taken in the hiring process. It may also include viewing an electronic portfolio that includes

© KONINKLIJKE BRILL NV, LEIDEN, 2018 | DOI 10.1163/9789004364486_014

lesson plans, student work samples, and video clips of teaching. To increase the likelihood of finding the right person to join an educational family and professional faculty, multiple interviews may occur, involving teammates and other teachers with whom the candidate will work. Sometimes the decision-making process includes an opportunity to watch a potential future colleague teach or interact with students. Finding the right match for the community, parents, peers, students, and principal is key to successful hiring that will last across time. Evidence of applicant's knowledge and skills may be uncovered through these processes. The assessment of an applicant's dispositions can be informed by using the DIA model and tools.

The building level principal may also use the DIA model to work towards building a learning community through establishing a shared mission and vision with and among teachers in the school. Their dispositions frame how teachers view and interpret mission statements and building level goals. Stark differences in *Dispositions in Action* (very responsive teachers working with very technical ones) can offer challenges to teachers working together closely, as on a team or in an inclusion setting. Understanding how dispositional differences are evidenced in classroom practice may provide another consideration when making decisions about team assignments and department and grade level placements of teachers. If teachers have a common language and model of dispositions, it aids those who work together to set goals for themselves and for collaboration with others. It may also give insight into another teacher's instructional decision-making and actions with others. Giving teachers language and tools to examine their dispositions and how this affects learning may help to build a better learning community with an increased focus on mutual understanding and joint ownership in important building level goals.

2   DIA for Teacher Preparation Programs

The *Dispositions in Action* model can be used in teacher preparation programs in several ways, including admissions screening, self-selection of whether to become an educator, or to counsel individuals out of the choice to teach when appropriate. Explicit teaching and cultivation of dispositions are typically lacking and sorely needed in teacher education. Using a model and approach that directly connects with and is evidenced in teaching practices allows dispositional standards to have meaning beyond philosophical musings and also identify potentially problematic candidate attitudes. The DIA model can also facilitate communication with partner schools around this important and typically most common reasons for teacher candidates struggling in their field experiences. Further, matching of mentors or supervising teachers with interns and student teachers who have similar dispositions increases the likelihood of candidate success in the school and classroom settings (Thornton, 2005). Standards and related accreditation may become more meaningfully and organically represented within a teacher preparation program. Connections can be made to other standard sets with the focus on student learning. The elusive, complex and potentially controversial nature of educator dispositions should not prohibit them from intentionally becoming a major component of curriculum and instruction within teacher education. DIA can help.

3   DIA for Teachers

In addition to being useful for administrators working with teachers to establish a sense of community and common vision, *Dispositions in Action* can be useful to teachers as individual professionals. Self-assessment of dispositions and creation of related professional development can be useful for those who seek to become responsively disposed. A mismatch of teacher dispositions among colleagues who work closely together is problematic. The teacher who finds herself teaching in a school environment that runs the opposite to her dispositions will likely have difficulty due to the tension between her dispositions and required teaching decisions and school norms. An assessment of *Dispositions in Action* can be helpful in examining levels of job satisfaction and reasons for not being satisfied. Further, assessment of *Dispositions in Action* may help a teacher in choosing to accept or decline a teaching position. She can be thoughtful of the alignment of the position with her dispositions and consider her willingness to address the challenges that may occur if there is a dispositional mismatch. As teachers work with colleagues on grade level teams, interdisciplinary teams, or as departments in the high school, dispositional matching comes into play just as it does for supervising student teachers. Learning how to understand your own dispositions in comparison to those of others can foster better communication between peers. Relationships are key to all of the teacher's interactions with colleagues, students, parents, and community. Understanding how your dispositions come to life within your classroom interactions may give insight into how your dispositions affect relationships with others overall.

4   DIA for Parents

Parents might also be interested in the concept of a teacher's *Dispositions in Action*. Just as goodness of fit is important to colleagues working together, it is also important to students working with their teachers. Dispositions are not set in stone. They are not blatantly dichotomous, but can rather be thought of as lying along a continuum between technical and responsive. Further, a teacher may be more technical in her disposition towards classroom management and responsive in her approach towards instruction. Understanding your child's personality tendencies, and how he or she may best work with teachers of specific dispositional orientations, can increase student success. It may also serve as a springboard for conversations with a teacher who is willing to engage in self-examination and developing dispositions that lead to meaningful student learning. Discussing dispositions with your child may also enable him or her to develop strategies that are useful in working with different kinds of people, whom they will certainly encounter in their lives in and outside of school. Parents or guardians are both the primary experts and advocates for their children. Understanding how dispositions affect interactions within the classroom may help the parent to problem solve with the teacher as her partner, rather than taking a more adversarial or passive role in making decisions for their child.

5   Tools to Get "IT"

As discussed previously in this book, the complex and less tangible standards for teacher dispositions and lack of consensus on a clear definition have been problematic. The *Dispositions in Action* concept may be a way to evaluate and cultivate dispositions that considers the direct relation between teacher dispositions and student learning. One of the best ways to gather data about teachers' *Dispositions in Action* is to take observational field notes of one's teaching. Ultimately, the use of field notes led to the identification of the themes and categories within the tools provided in this section. These tools may enable one to make an abstract concept more concrete, while still acknowledging its complexity and needed authenticity. The window to assess *Dispositions in Action* can be found in teachers' language, interactions and decision-making, as they determine how teaching and learning come to life with students. *Self-evaluative narratives* have been useful in enabling teachers to examine their own thinking related to the *Dispositions in Action* model and to set future dispositional goals. The forced choice *self-evaluation tool* helps teachers to identify their potential dispositional patterns and may serve as a starting point for conversations about types of *Dispositions in Action* and how they are present within and demonstrated by individuals. The *observation scale* enables a numerical value to be assigned to patterns of behaviors that represent responsive dispositions in the classroom. It further enables an examination across the domains of teaching for teachers to explore how they may be disposed similarly or differently across domains such as assessment, instruction, management, and professionalism. The *observation scale* is also useful to mentor and support supervising teachers in the field working with teacher candidates. It gives teacher mentors concrete evidence that may allow them to talk about more abstract and complex concepts with their peers and their mentees in a more thoughtful and analytical way. This observation tool can also be used for accountability purposes to collect data and evidence about the impact of teacher preparation on the development of dispositions. The *student interview guide* is useful in attempting to understand students' perceptions of teachers' dispositions and how they are evidenced in the classroom. It is helpful for classroom teachers to get the perspectives of these people that know them best as teachers, to gather information for professional reflection and growth. Combining these tools and processes provides multiple lenses by which to assess and examine teacher *Dispositions in Action*. These tools and examples are included below.

6   Self-evaluation Narratives

(What type of learning do I want and how do I align with that)

One tool that can begin to get teachers to think about their own *Dispositions in Action* is a reflective narrative. Prior to composing a narrative teachers may want to read articles about dispositions in general and specifically *Dispositions in Action* whenever possible. Discussion about and familiarity with the *Dispositions in Action* model is important to a successful reflection and self-evaluation. The teachers are prompted to respond to the question, "How am I responsive and how am I technical?" through use of the DIA model. Examples of these reflections follow.

Disposition Reflection Self-Analysis A

After reading the article on Dispositions in Action, *I found myself thinking of ways in which I have exhibited both responsive and technical dispositions. When I graduated from undergraduate school and went directly into teaching as a lateral entry teacher, with no formal educational background to teaching, I remember the teacher who came to be my "replacement mentor" because the mentor who was assigned to me was never present or communicated with me, giving me a WebQuest to give to the students to complete. This WebQuest was designed to get students to learn more about the organelles of the cell such as their function* (even though we talked about them in class) and how they look. This "mentor" told me to give the students the entire block to complete the assignment and if they did not finish it then "oh well, grade it anyway." I was shocked after hearing her instructions. I was teaching high school biology with 90 minute class periods and I remember asking her, "What if the students need more time and are diligently working?" Her response was, "Well let those students finish it for homework." I felt so confused and did not think that was very fair, but I went along with it because she did have more experience than me and she was nationally board certified. Upon reflection of this situation, I believe she had gradually allowed herself to let go of her teaching philosophy and had just "gone with the flow" of what administration wanted. By giving the students this WebQuest, I wasn't teaching them anything and they weren't learning anything by just copying what they saw on the computer screen and filling in the blanks. Since this was within my first month of teaching, I felt that I had no room to question a nationally board certified teacher. This is definitely an example of a technical disposition with being repetitive in instruction and controlling in management.

An example of how I was exhibiting a responsive disposition was when I was teaching high school students about simple and complex machines in physical science. I taught this class at a very small private school where students had significant academic and behavioral differences. Once the students learned about the different types of simple machines, such as their names and their functions, the students' performance task (which is not the phrase I would have used at the time) was for them to construct a complex machine to perform a task. It was modeled after the Rube Goldberg machine where you take a simple task and over simplify it. I created the rubric for the students, which gave them certain criteria to meet, such as using a certain number of simple machines, being able to explain how each component worked to accomplish the task, and their complex machine had to work. I gave students a variety of objects they could use to construct their machine and encouraged them to bring in items from home. I left the creativity aspect up to the students.

I also asked the students if they preferred to work independently or in groups. I was cautious about how the grouping would work because there were an odd number of students in the class, if the students were to choose this route. There were three girls and two boys. In my mind, I had a feeling of what groups would be created and I was correct, but the way they occurred was for the best. One of the boys and one of the girls paired up with each other, while two girls paired up. The other boy who was left out was kindly invited into both groups and he stated that he was more comfortable working by himself. I knew that he was making a good decision by working by himself instead of in a group because of his nature.

According to the dispositions table, I was exhibiting the "empowering" aspect of management because I asked for the students' input in their groupings and *allowed them to decide how they felt they would work best to complete the task. Another part of this assignment was for students to write daily journal entries describing the progress they made, how they felt working with their partner, or for the lone male student, how he felt he was doing working alone. I also made sure to conference with each group and the male student to better understand their ideas and thought processes. All of the students struggled in some aspect throughout the project and asked for my input, but I guided them to think for themselves, to ask their partner, or their classmates to emphasize problem solving skills. In the beginning, the students wanted me to give them a solution, but I did not give into that temptation. This also established a sense of trust between the students as they asked for advice and the student had to determine if he/she wanted to implement that suggestion. I also encouraged all of the students and reminded them that they were given a tough, but not impossible task. The end results were great and the students were proud of their machines and everyone's worked. They all reflected well about their experience and not only could I see their problem solving happening in real time, but through their reflections, they explicitly communicated how they learned to compromise, work together, and problem solve. For the student who worked by himself, he communicated that he became frustrated because he didn't have a partner to rely on but he did allow himself to ask for help from his peers although I could tell it hurt his pride to do so.*

I have used the "facilitative" disposition during class discussions about science related topics, such as cloning. I have used probing questions about the ethical concerns involved with cloning, as well as provided different scenarios to get students wondering if cloning is a good idea but maybe only for certain purposes. After providing the students with these thought provoking questions, the students began asking each other questions about the topics and began to challenge each other's perspectives.

I think this model helped me understand my dispositions and has given me a different perspective of how I can relinquish the control that I want to have in my classroom because of my A-type personality. One way in which I learned to relinquish that control is when I demonstrated the change-driven aspect of the responsive disposition during a few times throughout the school year when I taught middle and high school physical science. There were times when I planned for a particular lesson to go one way, but the students would make suggestions about doing things differently. I remember telling the students that it wasn't what I planned, but we could give their suggestions a try and see what happened. I have to admit that I am one that likes to be in control, but I knew that it would be for my student's best interest to be open to their suggestions. After doing the reading and this reflection, I feel that I am becoming more confident in how I can be more responsive to my students and how I have had glimpses of this particular disposition in my previous teaching experience.

Disposition Reflection Self Analysis B

I found the readings on dispositions very interesting because it is something that I think about a lot in my own life, both personal and professional. I think our dispositions affect every aspect of our lives from our personal relationships to our professional success and our everyday happiness or discontent. It makes so much sense to me that a person's dispositions would also affect his/her effectiveness as a teacher. Several of the dispositions resonated with me and my experience teaching one year of 9th grade back in 2003 and my current job as a teaching assistant in the 3rd grade. I definitely fall more towards the Responsive side of the chart in all classroom functions. As far as Assessment goes, I probably fall in the Challenging category. I am always working to develop more elements from the Critical disposition as well. I have to admit that there are some students that I will sometimes show more of an Accepting disposition towards—not in terms of low expectations, but in terms of effort and compliance. Those are the students that have diagnosed attention issues, and I do find it a challenge to maintain high expectations on days when they do not take their medicine. However, I know they have the ability to be engaged learners and it is so rewarding when I figure out the way to get them involved in learning even on their "off" days.

For Instruction, I am both Facilitative and Creative. I love making connections to students' lives and seeing them light up when that connection really hits home for them. I have felt a shift in my actions during my short time as a teaching assistant this school year from one of "giving answers" to guiding inquiry. I have strengthened that skill of guiding over the last few months, and it brings so much more joy to me as a teacher and to my students when they find the answer "on their own." The teachers I assist are experts at this, and it has been a great experience for me to learn the art of inquiry from them.

*My disposition in Management tends toward Empowering with some Connected as well. I love getting students involved in managing **their** classroom, and they enjoy it as well. I encourage students to problem-solve, and I model problem-solving and conflict resolution skills in my day-to-day activities in class. I recognize students as individuals and have gotten very good at identifying their unique interests and tying those interests into what we're learning.*

Finally, in terms of Professionalism, my disposition is to be both Change-driven and Inclusive. I am extremely interested and involved in professional growth for myself, which is appropriate for my stage as a new teacher. I hope to eventually lend my time and talents to improving education as a whole, adding to the research in the field, and also advocating best practices on a state and federal level. I believe in collaboration and multiple voices and perspectives on all topics, but particularly on the topic of education, which is so vital to every person and every aspect of our society. My disposition toward inclusivity informs my change-driven outlook.

I believe the Dispositions in Action *model is very strong and all facets are well supported with sound evidence. I am glad to now have language that I can apply to the feelings that I already had about my personal beliefs and mindset and how those can impact my teaching.*

Disposition Reflection Self Analysis C

In terms of assessment: *Overall, I think I lean toward the responsive model in terms of assessing students; however, there are aspects of the technical model that I think are important to assessing mathematics. It will be important for me to assess students in a way that is probing with an emphasis on deeper understanding of the material and success for all students. I plan to consistently assess students on how to transfer their learnings to real world applications (for example, the formative assessment that asks students to apply learnings on equivalent ratios to create a recipe converter). Some aspects of the technical disposition are also important for mathematics such as a focus on correctness and completion of tasks because students must fully understand the fundamental building block needed to understand higher mathematical concepts. I don't think I will put an emphasis on grades but I will strive for all students to reach proficiency before moving to the next set of learning objectives. I plan to be both focused on the journey and the end result of reaching proficiency.*

In terms of instruction: *Overall, I think I lean toward the responsive model in terms of instructing students; however, there are aspects of the technical model that I think are important to instructing mathematics. I mostly plan to play to role of facilitator where I can guide students and toward a more self-directed learning environment. I plan to do this by incorporating student-led learnings where the students can work collaboratively to gain deeper understanding of the learning objectives. I will be there to asking guiding questions to help students achieve this goal instead of giving students direct answers. I do think that there are aspects of the technical model that will be important in the initial stages teaching new mathematical learning objectives, such as covering facts and using repetition to enforce skills. For example, I plan to use online tools and worksheets to cover the fundamental building blocks and concepts. I still plan to present this material in a student-led, engaging way. Once the students have reached proficiency using the more technical model, the students will then be asked to* *apply those learnings in a collaborative learning environment which will align more to the responsive model.*

In terms of management: *Overall, I think I lean toward the responsive model in terms of managing students; however, there are aspects of the technical model that I think are important to managing students in the classroom. I definitely plan to engage students in the development of learning activities and assessments that they think will best help them achieve the learning objectives. I definitely plan to manage my classroom with an emphasis on fairness and equity for all students where I am responsive to the varied learning and developmental needs of each individual student. I also think that there are aspect of the technical model that are important to effectively managing a classroom. I do think that there should be a set of classroom guidelines for appropriate behavior and interaction that should be developed collaboratively with the students so we are all on board with certain expectations. I do not plan to address infractions with punishment, but plan to engage in a dialogue with students on why the behavior is not supporting our common goals as a classroom and how they can modify this behavior in the future. I also plan to incorporate activities such as mindfulness and intention. For example, start each class with a mindfulness activity that helps them focus on the upcoming unit and ask each student to set an individual intention for the unit (i.e.: try to pay attention, listen to other points of view, don't be afraid to express my point of view, etc.)*

Closing thoughts regarding technical versus responsive disposition in the classroom: *I don't think that there is a "one size fits all model" that I should adopt in the classroom. I think that I will mostly lean toward the responsive model but the technical model has its value as evidenced by my self-evaluation. Like everything in life, there are a lot of grey areas that have to be navigated on a situational basis using intuition and experience.*

These reflective analyses give insight into each teacher's understanding of the concept of dispositions and the *Dispositions in Action* model, as well as how they see it relating to instructional choices in the classroom. Reading these analyses also indicates where teachers might be more technically disposed. Further, providing explanations from their practice or daily lives helps to round out their own pictures of teacher dispositions.

7   **Multiple Choice Word Preference Scale**

The *Disposition in Action* word preference scale is provided to teachers with instructions to choose between two words, the word they prefer the most.

Participants indicate their degree of preference using the sliding scale by putting an X where they would place themselves in the preference continuum. Participants are instructed not to overthink or overanalyze the words and their potential meanings. Instead, they should indicate their gut reactions and quickly decide their preference between the two words provided. The word preference scale tool includes five choices for each of the identified teaching domains including assessment, instruction, management, and professionalism for total of twenty choices.

Disposition in Action Word Preference Scale

Choose which of the two words you prefer. Decide your level of preference. Indicate by placing an X over the box.

1. pursue   *satisfy*

| Strongly Prefer | Prefer | Prefer | Strongly Prefer |

2. understand   *accomplish*

| Strongly Prefer | Prefer | Prefer | Strongly Prefer |

3. success   *effort*

| Strongly Prefer | Prefer | Prefer | Strongly Prefer |

4. fairness   *rules*

| Strongly Prefer | Prefer | Prefer | Strongly Prefer |

5. creative   *reliable*

| Strongly Prefer | Prefer | Prefer | Strongly Prefer |

6. experimental   *verified*

| Strongly Prefer | Prefer | Prefer | Strongly Prefer |

7. asking   *telling*

Strongly Prefer   Prefer   Prefer   Strongly Prefer

8. explore   *complete*

Strongly Prefer   Prefer   Prefer   Strongly Prefer

9. varied   *consistent*

Strongly Prefer   Prefer   Prefer   Strongly Prefer

10. relative   *equal*

Strongly Prefer   Prefer   Prefer   Strongly Prefer

11. relationship   *respect*

Strongly Prefer   Prefer   Prefer   Strongly Prefer

12. flexibility   *order*

Strongly Prefer   Prefer   Prefer   Strongly Prefer

13. thorough   *efficient*

Strongly Prefer   Prefer   Prefer   Strongly Prefer

14. collaborative   *individual*

Strongly Prefer   Prefer   Prefer   Strongly Prefer

15. free-reign   *boundaries*

| Strongly Prefer | Prefer | Prefer | Strongly Prefer |

16. empower   *command*

| Strongly Prefer | Prefer | Prefer | Strongly Prefer |

17. individualized   *standardized*

| Strongly Prefer | Prefer | Prefer | Strongly Prefer |

18. challenge   *reward*

| Strongly Prefer | Prefer | Prefer | Strongly Prefer |

19. change accept

| Strongly Prefer | Prefer | Prefer | Strongly Prefer |

20. innovation   *tradition*

| Strongly Prefer | Prefer | Prefer | Strongly Prefer |

Scoring guide

Example:
1. pursue satisfy

Points	4	3	2	1
	Strongly Prefer	Prefer	Prefer	Strongly Prefer

Each question is scored using the order above, with 4 scores on the left and 1 scores on the right.

Assessment Domain Questions: 1, 3, 2, 13, 17
Instructional Domain Questions: 5, 6, 7, 8, 9
Management Domain Questions: 4, 10, 11, 12, 16
Professional Domain Questions: 14, 15, 18, 19, 20

8   DIA Observation Tool

Emergent themes were identified throughout the research and observations of *Dispositions in Action* to enable observations to become more focused, more clearly defined, and to enable establishment of inter-rater reliability. These themes are found in the DIA observation tool. Within the assessment domain, identified themes are expectations, understanding, questioning, and methods. Looking at specific descriptors within each theme helps evaluators to determine the level of responsiveness with multiple lenses, within each domain. Themes within the instructional domain are individualization, conceptual understanding, developmental responsiveness, relevance, multiple paths to understanding and feedback. The management domain includes decision-making, curriculum and instruction, classroom observations, student rapport individual management and classroom management.

TABLE 14.1 *Responsive DIA Observation.*

Teacher: _____

Observer: _____

Subject(s)/content area(s): _____

Date: _____

Responsive interaction within assessment (challenging/critical)

Indicators of dispositions via dialogue high level of responsiveness (3)	Indicators of dispositions via dialogue medium level of responsiveness (2)	Indicators of dispositions via dialogue low level of responsiveness (1)	Score/comments
Expectations: The teacher regularly talks with students and interacts with them in ways that authentically communicate high expectations for learning.	*Expectations:* The teacher indicates that some students are capable of meeting high expectations while others are not as capable.	*Expectations:* The teacher talks with students and interacts with them in ways that emphasize effort and compliance as success.	
Understanding: Dialogue and interaction regularly encourage deeper levels of understanding and emphasize progress toward high quality performances of understanding.	*Understanding:* Dialogue and interaction go beyond the "givens" of the task toward higher levels of thinking.	*Understanding:* Dialogue and interaction focus on completion of tasks and assignments with little probing or questioning to move beyond the "givens" of the task.	

TABLE 14.1 *Responsive DIA Observation (cont.).*

Responsive interaction within assessment (challenging/critical)

Indicators of dispositions via dialogue high level of responsiveness (3)	Indicators of dispositions via dialogue medium level of responsiveness (2)	Indicators of dispositions via dialogue low level of responsiveness (1)	Score/ comments
Questioning: Dialogue and interaction focus on questioning and probing to reveal the students' depth of understanding to move beyond surface assumptions and statements of "facts," often seeking students' opinions, or justifications and reasoning behind responses.	*Questioning:* Dialogue and interactions typically center on teacher questions that focus on seeking the correct answer to a question or set of questions, with occasional follow up to check for student understanding.	*Questioning:* Dialogue and interaction center on the teacher typically providing information, with limited focus on questioning students or student questions.	
Methods of assessment: Assessment of learning (both formative and summative) occurs regularly within the flow of student/student/teacher interactions throughout instruction and is used to set goals for students and to guide further learning.	*Methods of assessment:* Assessment of learning occurs in pre-determined projects, activities or assignments and is primarily of a summative nature, with occasional informal checks for understanding.	*Methods of assessment:* Assessment takes place almost exclusively separate from instruction (usually post) using methods such as tests and quizzes.	

Responsive interaction within instruction (facilitative/creative)

Indicators of dispositions via dialogue high level (3)	Indicators of dispositions via dialogue medium level (2)	Indicators of dispositions via dialogue low level (1)	Score/comments
Individualization: The teacher frequently responds to student questions, notes their progress, and incorporates their ideas, experiences and interests into instruction.	*Individualization:* The teacher responds to student questions, progress, and ideas and occasionally builds this into instruction.	*Individualization:* The teacher emphasizes one approach to learning for all students.	
Conceptual understanding: Lessons regularly feature the scaffolding of skills and concepts to build on students' current understanding and questions to obtain deeper levels of understanding including synthesis and evaluation	*Conceptual understanding:* Lessons occasionally vary the explanation of concepts and the performance of skills in response to students' questions, typically focused an application level of understanding.	*Conceptual understanding:* Lessons emphasize the explanation of concepts in a prescribed order typically focused on a recall level of understanding.	

TABLE 14.1   *Responsive DIA Observation (cont.).*

Responsive interaction within instruction (facilitative/creative)

Indicators of dispositions via dialogue high level (3)	Indicators of dispositions via dialogue medium level (2)	Indicators of dispositions via dialogue low level (1)	Score/comments
Developmental responsiveness: The teacher talks and interacts with students in ways that indicate responsiveness to individual differences in developmental needs.	*Developmental responsiveness:* The teacher talks and interacts with students in ways that show some awareness of individual differences in developmental needs.	*Developmental responsiveness:* The teacher talks with students and interacts with them in ways that are not developmentally responsive and are often the same from class to class and situation to situation and student to student.	
Relevance: The teacher regularly relates classroom learning experiences to real world situations and makes connections to students' lives beyond school.	*Relevance:* The teacher occasionally relates classroom learning experiences to real world situations and makes connections to students' lives beyond school.	*Relevance:* The teacher talks with students and interacts with them in ways that emphasize the coverage of information. Any connections beyond the classroom are incidental.	

Responsive interaction within instruction (facilitative/creative)

Indicators of dispositions via dialogue high level (3)	Indicators of dispositions via dialogue medium level (2)	Indicators of dispositions via dialogue low level (1)	Score/comments
Multiple paths to understanding: The teacher encourages multiple ways of demonstrating depth of understanding within and after instruction	*Multiple paths to understanding:* The teacher offers may offer multiple opportunities for student demonstration of understanding primarily after instruction.	*Multiple paths to understanding:* The teacher emphasizes a single pathway to learning and assessing whether or not students demonstrate prescribed skills and procedures after instruction.	
Feedback: The teacher regularly provides multiple forms of feedback to students to guide the growth of their understanding during instruction, building on and challenging students' conceptual understanding.	*Feedback:* The teacher occasionally provides feedback to students during instruction, primarily focused on addressing students' misconceptions.	*Feedback:* The teacher generally limits feedback to grades on assignments, with only corrective feedback during instruction.	

TABLE 14.1   *Responsive DIA Observation* (*cont.*).

Responsive interaction with students (empowering/connected)

Indicators of dispositions via dialogue high level (3)	Indicators of dispositions via dialogue medium level (2)	Indicators of dispositions via dialogue low level (1)	Score/comments
Decision making: The teacher regularly seeks input from students related to instructional strategies, assessment and the focus of the curriculum and instruction in the classroom.	*Decision making:* The teacher occasionally involves students in instructional decisions by giving options within assignments or projects.	*Decision making:* The teacher focuses on covering information and material with very few adjustments made related to student feedback or input.	
Curriculum and instruction: The teacher elicits student questions and interpretation of learning to gain data to inform future plans related to aspects of classroom curriculum and instruction.	*Curriculum and instruction:* The teacher gives students some choices about what to learn and how to learn.	*Curriculum and instruction:* The teacher rarely seeks feedback from students related to curriculum and instruction.	
Classroom expectations: Structure and organization in classroom supports dialogue and interaction with individuals and groups of students in running the classroom.	*Classroom expectations:* Students have some choices regarding classroom procedures.	*Classroom expectations:* The teacher talks with students and interacts with them in ways that emphasize following directions, rules and completing tasks.	

Responsive interaction with students (empowering/connected)

Indicators of dispositions via dialogue high level (3)	Indicators of dispositions via dialogue medium level (2)	Indicators of dispositions via dialogue low level (1)	Score/comments
Student rapport: Student dialogue with each other and teacher is truly collaborative with a focus on quality and mutual support in setting and attaining goals and personal support.	*Student rapport:* Classroom conversations indicate a congenial, cooperative atmosphere with some student interaction to achieve learning goals	*Student rapport:* Teacher talk rarely veers from focus on "given" content and coverage of this content with limited student interaction.	
Individual management: The teacher talks with students and interacts with them in ways that show "withitness" and keen awareness of individual students, and flexibility in responding to each student..	*Individual management:* The teacher talks with students and interacts with them in ways that show some awareness of individual differences and some variation in responding to students.	*Individual management:* The teacher talks with students and interacts with them in ways that center on maintaining consistency and authority in responding to students.	
Classroom management: The teacher proactively addresses disruptions and promotes student engagement in ways that encourage shared responsibility and a sense of community and intrinsic motivation. The focus is on student problem solving.	*Classroom management:* The teacher addresses disruptions and promotes student engagement in ways that primarily emphasize extrinsic motivation. The focus is on "on task" behavior.	*Classroom management:* Teacher addresses disruptions and promotes engagement in primarily autocratic ways The focus is on individual compliance to class rules and norms.	

TABLE 14.1   *Responsive DIA Observation (cont.).*

Responsive interaction with students (empowering/connected)

Indicators of dispositions via dialogue high level (3)	Indicators of dispositions via dialogue medium level (2)	Indicators of dispositions via dialogue low level (1)	Score/comments
Decision making: The teacher regularly seeks input from students related to instructional strategies, assessment and the focus of the curriculum and instruction in the classroom.	*Decision making:* The teacher occasionally involves students in instructional decisions by giving options within assignments or projects.	*Decision making:* The teacher focuses on covering information and material with very few adjustments made related to student feedback or input.	2.5 – Giving multiple choices of assignments to complete (3) allows students freedom of expression and gives students ownership over assessment. Curriculum is still very much teacher-led (2).
Curriculum and instruction: The teacher elicits student questions and interpretation of learning to gain data to inform future plans related to aspects of classroom curriculum and instruction.	*Curriculum and instruction:* The teacher gives students some choices about what to learn and how to learn.	*Curriculum and instruction:* The teacher rarely seeks feedback from students related to curriculum and instruction.	3 – The teacher gives students multiple choices of how to apply learned material and also uses such applications and products to shape future curriculum and instruction (3).

Responsive interaction with students (empowering/connected)

Indicators of dispositions via dialogue high level (3)	Indicators of dispositions via dialogue medium level (2)	Indicators of dispositions via dialogue low level (1)	Score/comments
Classroom expectations: Structure and organization in classroom supports dialogue and interaction with individuals and groups of students in running the classroom.	*Classroom expectations:* Students have some choices regarding classroom procedures.	*Classroom expectations:* The teacher talks with students and interacts with them in ways that emphasize following directions, rules and completing tasks,	2.75 – Students only have choice regarding application of learned content (2), but lesson/classroom planning and organization supports group discussion among students and with teacher (3).
Student rapport: Student dialogue with each other and teacher is truly collaborative with a focus on quality and mutual support in setting and attaining goals and personal support.	*Student rapport:* Classroom conversations indicate a congenial, cooperative atmosphere with some student interaction to achieve learning goals	*Student rapport:* Teacher talk rarely veers from focus on "given" content and coverage of this content with limited student interaction.	2.25 – Student dialogue within groups is primarily focused on achieving success within the parameters of the class (2) less about mutual support and growth in general, however this is more the case with more advanced classes (3).

TABLE 14.1   *Responsive DIA Observation (cont.).*

Responsive interaction with students (empowering/connected)

Indicators of dispositions via dialogue high level (3)	Indicators of dispositions via dialogue medium level (2)	Indicators of dispositions via dialogue low level (1)	Score/comments
Individual management: The teacher talks with students and interacts with them in ways that show "withitness" and keen awareness of individual students, and flexibility in responding to each student. The focus is on student problem solving.	*Individual management:* The teacher talks with students and interacts with them in ways that show some awareness of individual differences and some variation in responding to students.	*Individual management:* The teacher talks with students and interacts with them in ways that center on maintaining consistency and authority in responding to students.	2.75 – Teacher responds to students based on individual level of development and achievement (3) but finds slight difficulty reaching each student during independent work sessions – which is to be expected. (2)
Classroom management: The teacher proactively addresses disruptions and promotes student engagement in ways that encourage shared responsibility and a sense of community and intrinsic motivation. The focus is on student problem solving.	*Classroom management:* The teacher addresses disruptions and promotes student engagement in ways that primarily emphasize extrinsic motivation. The focus is on "on task" behavior.	*Classroom management:* Teacher addresses disruptions and promotes engagement in primarily autocratic ways The focus is on individual compliance to class rules and norms.	2.5 – Although focus is primarily on on-task behavior (2)," the teacher has created an environment that does not lead to problems, other than general distractions (3) – most students are focused on completing the task at hand and learning the content. The presence of an observer is a main distraction, but otherwise students can distract one another.

Responsive interaction within assessment (challenging/critical)

Indicators of dispositions via dialogue high level (3)	Indicators of dispositions via dialogue medium level (2)	Indicators of dispositions via dialogue low level (1)	Score/comments
Expectations: The teacher regularly talks with students and interacts with them in ways that authentically communicate high expectations for learning.	*Expectations:* The teacher indicates that some students are capable of meeting high expectations while others are not as capable.	*Expectations:* The teacher talks with students and interacts with them in ways that emphasize effort and compliance as success.	2.75 – Teacher expresses high expectations for student performance for all students (3), but understands that some students are not at the same developmental level as others in the class – differentiation (2). Shows belief that all students can achieve.
Understanding: Dialogue and interaction regularly encourage deeper levels of understanding and emphasize progress toward high quality performances of understanding.	*Understanding:* Dialogue and interaction go beyond the "givens" of the task toward higher levels of thinking.	*Understanding:* Dialogue and interaction focus on completion of tasks and assignments with little probing or questioning to move beyond the "givens" of the task.	2.75 – Dialogue during group interpretations of current events is focused primarily on understanding one aspect of the article (2), but group discussion pulls in other aspects, scaffolding thought about the subject to deeper levels (3). During independent group work, dialogue between teacher and students pushes students to think more in-depth about the content to create high-quality products that demonstrate level of understanding (3).

TABLE 14.1   *Responsive DIA Observation (cont.).*

Responsive interaction within assessment (challenging/critical)

Indicators of dispositions via dialogue high level (3)	Indicators of dispositions via dialogue medium level (2)	Indicators of dispositions via dialogue low level (1)	Score/comments
Questioning: Dialogue and interaction focus on questioning and probing to reveal the students' depth of understanding to move beyond surface assumptions and statements of "facts," often seeking students' opinions, or justifications and reasoning behind responses.	*Questioning:* Dialogue and interactions typically center on teacher questions that focus on seeking the correct answer to a question or set of questions, with occasional follow up to check for student understanding.	*Questioning:* Dialogue and interaction centers on the teacher typically providing information, with limited focus on questioning students or student questions.	2.25 – Dialogue and questioning is generally focused on seeking the correct answer to questions about the topic (2). Although probing for deeper understanding, the true depth of thought is only expressed in independent work (3), and could be pushed for a bit more in terms of students' opinions and thoughts on certain topics.
Methods of assessment: Assessment of learning (both formative and summative) occurs regularly within the flow of student/student/ teacher interactions throughout instruction and is used to set goals for students and to guide further learning.	*Methods of assessment:* Assessment of learning occurs in pre-determined projects, activities or assignments and is primarily of a summative nature, with occasional informal checks for understanding.	*Methods of assessment:* Assessment takes place almost exclusively separate from instruction (usually post) using methods such as tests and quizzes.	2.5 – assessment of learning is a blend of formative and summative, which occurs regularly (3), however the formative assessments are generally more informal than formal (2) with the summative assessments (i.e. activities) providing the majority of assessment of student learning.

Responsive interaction within instruction (facilitative/creative)

Indicators of dispositions via dialogue high level (3)	Indicators of dispositions via dialogue medium level (2)	Indicators of dispositions via dialogue low level (1)	Score/comments
Individualization: The teacher frequently responds to student questions, notes their progress, and incorporates their ideas, experiences and interests into instruction.	*Individualization:* The teacher responds to student questions, progress, and ideas and occasionally builds this into instruction.	*Individualization:* The teacher emphasizes one approach to learning for all students.	2.25 – Teacher responds to students questions, progress, and ideas and takes this into account when designing curriculum and instruction (3) but generally focuses on exposing students to experiences that are more relevant to content, rather than molding the content around their interests (2).
Conceptual understanding: Lessons regularly feature the scaffolding of skills and concepts to build on students' current understanding and questions to obtain deeper levels of understanding including synthesis and evaluation	*Conceptual understanding:* Lessons occasionally vary the explanation of concepts and the performance of skills in response to students' questions, typically focused an application level of understanding.	*Conceptual understanding:* Lessons emphasize the explanation of concepts in a prescribed order typically focused on a recall level of understanding.	2.5 – Lessons tend to provide students the opportunity to apply their learned skills and knowledge in a way that best demonstrates their own level of understanding (2), but also allows them to synthesize their learned skills and abilities to create a product that is best representative of their understanding of the subject (3).

TABLE 14.1　*Responsive DIA Observation (cont.).*

Responsive interaction within instruction (facilitative/creative)

Indicators of dispositions via dialogue high level (3)	Indicators of dispositions via dialogue medium level (2)	Indicators of dispositions via dialogue low level (1)	Score/comments
Developmental responsiveness: The teacher talks and interacts with students in ways that indicate responsiveness to individual differences in developmental needs.	*Developmental responsiveness:* The teacher talks and interacts with students in ways that show some awareness of individual differences in developmental needs.	*Developmental responsiveness:* The teacher talks with students and interacts with them in ways that are not developmentally responsive and are often the same from class to class and situation to situation and student to student.	2.5 – The teacher's interactions and discussions with students are responsive to their individual developmental levels (3), but could show some improvement on reaching the entire class such a level (2).
Relevance: The teacher regularly relates classroom learning experiences to real world situations and makes connections to students' lives beyond school.	*Relevance:* The teacher occasionally relates classroom learning experiences to real world situations and makes connections to students' lives beyond school.	*Relevance:* The teacher talks with students and interacts with them in ways that emphasize the coverage of information. Any connections beyond the classroom are incidental.	2.5 – The teacher makes an earnest attempt to connect classroom learning experiences to the world outside of school, particularly on an nation-wide and worldwide level (3), but such connections do not tend to directly relate to the lives of the students themselves (2).

Responsive interaction within instruction (facilitative/creative)

Indicators of dispositions via dialogue high level (3)	Indicators of dispositions via dialogue medium level (2)	Indicators of dispositions via dialogue low level (1)	Score/comments
Multiple paths to understanding: The teacher encourages multiple ways of demonstrating depth of understanding within and after instruction	*Multiple paths to understanding:* The teacher offers may offer multiple opportunities for student demonstration of understanding primarily after instruction.	*Multiple paths to understanding:* The teacher emphasizes a single pathway to learning and assessing whether or not students demonstrate prescribed skills and procedures after instruction.	2.25 – The teacher encourages multiple ways of demonstrating depth of understanding of the content (3), however, this primarily takes place as students complete the task after instruction (2)

TABLE 14.1   *Responsive DIA Observation (cont.).*

Responsive interaction within instruction (facilitative/creative)

Indicators of dispositions via dialogue high level (3)	Indicators of dispositions via dialogue medium level (2)	Indicators of dispositions via dialogue low level (1)	Score/comments
Feedback: The teacher regularly provides multiple forms of feedback to students to guide the growth of their understanding during instruction, building on and challenging students' conceptual understanding.	*Feedback:* The teacher occasionally provides feedback to students during instruction, primarily focused on addressing students' misconceptions.	*Feedback:* The teacher generally limits feedback to grades on assignments, with only corrective feedback during instruction.	2.5 – The teacher regularly provides feedback to guide students' learning during instruction (3), but could improve upon challenging students' understanding of concepts on a deeper level (2).

Comments – Overall, Ms. Wilson does a very good job of keeping her students engaged in the lesson and activity at hand. She has attempted created a culture of inquiry that will support learning beyond the classroom. She has used curricular topics to push student thinking outside their usual frame of perception in an attempt to widen their worldview and encourage thought beyond their daily lives.
Suggestions – Try pushing student thinking to deeper levels of understanding. Encourage connections between what is being presented in the lesson and other areas of interest (between scientific concepts, and between science and other content area concentrations). Also, try to establish explicit connections between the curriculum and students' direct experiences and interests, to make learning relevant and applicable to students' personal lives, as well as incorporating students' individual interests into your instruction.
Overall 2.6 out of 3

This tool is premised on the following assertions related to dispositions:

1 A basic dictionary definition of "disposition" is "one's customary frame of mind." For educational purposes we define dispositions as "teacher's habits of mind that shape ways that they interact with students and the ways they make decisions in the classroom."
2 Dispositions are evidenced through interaction with students and the kinds of dialogue observed in the classrooms.
3 Scores are between 3.0–1.0 with varying degrees including 3.0, 2.75, 2.5, 2.0, 1.75, 1.5, 1.0

Example
Teacher: Ms. Wilson
Observer: Mr. Gaines
Subject(s)/content area(s):   8th Grade Science
Date: April 12, 2016

9   Student Interview Guide

My dissertation study examining students' perspectives of school reform was actually the impetus for the development of the *Dispositions in Action* concept, as it led to a focus on the nature of teacher behaviors. The teacher's nature led to differences in learning, even when teachers were using the same approaches to curriculum and instruction. Studying these differences led to identifying and examining teacher dispositions, and subsequently the *Dispositions in Action* model. Listening to students' voices can provide valuable insight to teachers who want to reflect upon and improve their practices and classroom relationships. These guide questions may be used with individuals. They are often most informative and beneficial when used with small focus groups of four to six students, as students push each other to say and explain more as they build on or challenge other's responses. The members of the interview group may be intentionally selected depending on what the teacher is trying to find out. It may make sense to have a mix of kids from different abilities and backgrounds in a group. Or it may make sense to have a focus group that represents student characteristics that may be influencing your instructional decisions. Intentionality and close listening to students are vital to this interview process. After, an informal examination of answers should allow educators to notice trends and themes within and across the students' responses. If the findings need to be formal in nature, developing a coding system, as one would in qualitative analysis is helpful.

K-12 Student Interview Guide

– What does your teacher consider most important in the classroom? (This will give an overall indication of which domains the teacher emphasizes and show potential overall dispositional trends).

– How does your teacher know how well you are learning/understanding lessons? (This will give insight into assessment dispositions).

– How does your teacher most often (or like to) teach? Give specific examples. (This will give insight into instructional dispositions).

– What are your teacher's expectations of you? (This will give insight into management dispositions).

– What qualities make a good teacher? (This will give insight into students' needs/perspectives on dispositions and serve as an internal member check).

10   **Resources**

Identifying resources that may encourage discussion about teachers' *Dispositions in Action* should go beyond the educator disposition literature. Since *Dispositions in Action* concern themselves with what teachers actually do the classroom, it may be helpful to find examples of practices that typically align with responsive dispositions across the various domains. We know that teachers may employ the same teaching strategies, the same assessment tools, and the same curriculum but their dispositions can cause similar approaches to look and mean very different things across their classrooms. This means that mandating the use of or providing professional development about a specific approach or method does not assure the results in learning that the approach may logically seem to imply. Ultimately, the conversation should focus on what do dispositions look like and mean in teaching. Connections to teacher quality frameworks and teacher standards have been shared in previous chapters. This list of resources makes connections to constructs and practices which align with responsive and technical *Dispositions in Action*. Dispositions are not the focus of these resources, but rather exploring the resources with DIA in mind and using it to cultivate why level dialogue related to these approaches helps to reveal how dispositions affect and direct what teachers do in the classroom.

Think again:

1 What audience (administrators, teachers, professors, parents) do you think is best addressed using the DIA model? Why? Which would be problematic and why?

TABLE 14.2   *Responsive/technical related concepts.*

Responsive	Technical
Assessment:	*Assessment:*
Authentic assessment	Paper/pencil
Performance-based	Tests and quizzes
Essential questions	Text based questions
Backwards design	Homework
Proficiency	Letter grades
Formative	Summative
Instruction:	*Instruction:*
Teaching for understanding	Lecture
Differentiation	Direct instruction
Inquiry	Practice and drill
Collaboration	Facts and procedures
Makerspace	RTI (Response to Intervention)
Student-driven and integrated	Curriculum pacing guides
Curriculum	Individual work
DOK	Reading-based comprehension
Questioning	Memorization and recall
Problem-based instruction	
Management:	*Management:*
Class meetings	Zero tolerance
Peer mediation	School-wide rules
Engaged learning	Time on task
Intrinsic rewards	Quiet
Kohlberg's moral development	Assertive discipline/strike systems
Glasser's choice theory	PBIS (Positive Behavior Intervention
Democratic classrooms	System)
Mindfulness	Extrinsic rewards and punishment
Equal is not fair	Black and White
Proactive	Teacher as rule enforcer
	Same treatment for all
Professionalism:	*Professionalism:*
Teacher leadership	Principal led schools
Shared decision making	Top down decision making
Teaching against the grain	Accountability
Teacher as change agent	Preservation and tradition
Teaching and policy/politics	Teaching as apolitical

2 Which of the DIA tools do you think would be most useful? In what circumstances?
3 Discuss how you think the resources in the chart above fit the dispositions with which they are aligned and why. Is there an alignment that you would challenge or see differently?

Reference

Thornton, H. (2005). PDS master teacher selection: Inquiry and action using peer evaluation. In M. Caskey (Ed.), *The handbook of research in middle level education*. Greenwich, CT: Information Age Publishing.

CHAPTER 15

Next Steps for DIA: A Call to Action

Think about:

1 How can we use a focus on dispositions and DIA to benefit the educators and the students they teach?

•••

I was intrigued when I first encountered the notion of epistemology. Technically, epistemology is a branch of philosophy that examines the nature and origin of knowledge. It asks the question, "How do we know what we know?" My understanding of epistemology is that is has to do with one's worldview, how you think about the world in terms of reality versus perception, facts versus understanding, black and white versus gray. Is knowledge fixed, clear-cut, and representative of universal truths as in modernist thinking? Or instead, do people continually construct their own knowledge, thus knowledge inherently reflects particular perspectives and views? Modernism is related to positivism, which is the belief that there are absolute truths, facts and objectivity. The shift to a postmodern philosophy indicates a shift of focus to considering the lenses through which with we view "reality" such as individual lived experiences, societal constructs, and self-identities. Gergen (2010) states

The modernist perspective, as represented in the arts, sciences, and cultural life, is centrally concerned with locating foundational forms. This romance with essentials is manifest in psychology's assumption of a basic, knowable subject matter; universal psychological processes; truth by (empirical) method; and research as progressive. Yet, in broad sectors of the intellectual world—and elsewhere—one detects a defection from modernism and the emergence of a postmodern perspective. Dominant within postmodernism is a thoroughgoing perspectivism. All attempts at foundations are viewed, then, as reflections of particular perspectives, themselves without justification except by recourse to other perspectives.

A postmodern perspective begs for deeper analysis of what appears to be clearly factual by deconstructing ordinary experiences, words, and concepts to reveal their underlying perspectives and even how "facts" benefit certain groups' goals or objectives. This deeper analysis focuses on cultural, social, psychological, political, and historical impact on how we view and live in

© KONINKLIJKE BRILL NV, LEIDEN, 2018 | DOI 10.1163/9789004364486_015

our world. It acknowledges the need to look more deeply at what we assume and think more deeply about it in terms of seeking meaning. A postmodern perspective allows us to look more deeply into levels of understanding that go below the surface and are situated within the human experience. Postmodernism resonates with me. I have always been one to question, to seek the why level, and be interested in how others live their lives. This epistemology connected with my responsive dispositions in terms of being critical, challenging, and empowering. It definitely centers on the human and relational aspects of knowledge, as it goes beyond facts to examine why and how the facts exist.

Recently, I was listening to the radio on my way to work and I heard a discussion about postmodernism being replaced by an epistemology or worldview that the discussants were labeling "post-factual." The dictionary defines "post-factual," or post truth, as "relating to or denoting circumstances in which objective facts are less influential in shaping public opinion than appeals to emotion and personal belief." Facts are also questioned in postmodernism, but the questions are grounded in trying to understand other's perspectives and how we all make meaning of "factual information." In contrast, this new post factual questioning acts to negate the importance of facts that do not align with one's positions or beliefs. The emergence of the term "alternative facts" is not grounded in analysis of perspectives. It is not multifaceted, examining what affects and determines one's understanding of information and knowledge, but rather it ignores facts as a concept, suggesting that all opinions are equal, relevant, and should be heard and valued the in the same way. A post-factual worldview negates others' thoughts, questions scientific thinking and analysis, and lessens the chance of harmony, as it is an egocentric, self-centered and self-serving view of the world.

I would argue that dispositions are inherently linked to one's epistemology, or worldview. Much like postmodernism, which centers on meaning making and understanding people's perspectives, so too does post-factionalism. The difference is one is grounded in thinking, while the other is grounded in emotion. If we intend for education to result in students becoming competent, caring, and thinking individuals, we need teachers with responsive dispositions. Identifying, valuing, and teaching responsive dispositions offers an opportunity consider the means and ends of teacher preparation and professional development differently. It is an opportunity to intentionally acknowledge the importance of the human aspect of learning and the need to interact with others as we challenge and create new knowledge.

Teaching is a relational. It builds relationships between people and bridges to understanding facts and concepts. Teaching is about the very human side of our nature. We need to be mindful not to lose that in a world filled with technological innovation, that need not, but could, lead to the distancing of human interaction. Teaching is about modeling connections to others and developing empathy and critical thinking to build understanding and community, together. If we do not want to lose this focus in today's current context of uber-technology and increasing animosity between societal groups, we must be mindful of and intentional in addressing this concern.

In difficult times people ask, "How can we make the world better?" By making sure our students have the right kind of teachers to help them become the right kind of adults. Teaching is far more than content and pedagogical expertise and knowledge. It must focus on meaning making. Making sense of knowledge and concepts. Making sense of your own world and thoughts, making sense of others' perspectives and experiences, and making new meanings to move the world forward. If this is how we define teaching, we must find and cultivate teachers who are disposed to this definition and consider its implications for teacher decision-making and practice.

There is value in technical skill, expertise and dispositions. However, teaching is a human enterprise that goes far beyond technical prowess. We need not to let the focus on testing, accountability, finances, efficiency and technology dehumanize the act of teaching and learning. In order for teachers to help to create a better world for the future, they have to have the "It factor." "It" is the unique gift that teachers bring into the classroom to benefit their students and the good of society, and the world as a whole.

As our world becomes increasingly more virtual, we spend time watching others' realities instead of living in our own, creating our own truth rather than relying on evidence, and seeing relationships as drama infused and compromise as weakness. The technical has become accepted as more human than the human. We need to be disposed to be responsive to each other and the challenges and "new realities" of our world in a thoughtful, grounded way to move forward. Our students need to be disposed to think deeply. We need to work to more fully understand others and the world around us, but most importantly, to understand ourselves. Teachers have always wanted to change the world to move things forward. That is why they go into this profession. Our children can move us forward. Let us give them the best opportunity to do so by filling our classrooms with teachers who have this seemingly intangible "*It Factor*" that great teachers have. *It* can begin here with all of us.

Reference

Gergen, K. (2010). Toward a postmodern psychology. *The Human Psychologist, 18*(1), 23–34. Retrieved from http://dx.doi.org/10.1080/08873267.1990.9976874

Printed in the United States
By Bookmasters